WE ARE THE LEADERS
WE HAVE BEEN LOOKING FOR

The W. E. B. Du Bois Lectures

WE ARE THE LEADERS
WE HAVE BEEN LOOKING FOR

—

Eddie S. Glaude Jr.

Harvard University Press

Cambridge, Massachusetts & London, England   2024

First printing

Library of Congress Cataloging-in-Publication Data

Names: Glaude, Eddie S., Jr., 1968– author.

Title: We are the leaders we have been looking for / Eddie S. Glaude Jr.

Other titles: W. E. B. Du Bois lectures.

Description: Cambridge, Massachusetts : Harvard University Press, 2024. | Series: W. E. B. Du Bois lectures | Includes bibliographical references and index.

Identifiers: LCCN 2023039966 | ISBN 9780674737600 (cloth)

Subjects: LCSH: African Americans—Politics and government. | Political participation—United States. | Political leadership—United States. | Activism—United States. | Political activists—United States.

Classification: LCC E185.89.P6 G53 2024 | DDC 323/.0420973—dc23/eng/20230918

LC record available at https://lccn.loc.gov/2023039966

For my Dad

CONTENTS

— A Story —

OF THE FIVE BLACK MEN who made it to Heaven, one decided that he was going to try out the wings the angel Gabriel had given him. The other men told him to sit down and wait as Gabriel instructed them to do. Seated in golden chairs, they had received their robes and wings too. Heaven was their home now. A life of toil had been left behind. No need to disrupt things; simply wait until they were told what to do next. But one man insisted the wings were his, and he was going to use them. "Watch me skim around that tree of life without touching a leaf," he declared. "Watch me shoot right cross the Sea of Glass and around the throne and right 'cross God's nose without touching it. Just watch me." The others worried that he was going to knock over the delicate lamps and fine vases in Heaven as he darted back and forth. He did, eventually, and God didn't say a word. He just looked at him. Gabriel returned, angry, snatched off the man's wings, and told him, "Sit down until I tell you to move!" The other men chastised him and said, "Look, now everybody got wings but you." The man smiled and said, "I don't care. I sure was a flying fool when I had them."[1]

This folktale from Zora Neale Hurston's fieldwork on the Gulf Coast is a different kind of story of Black people who could fly. Typically, the tales center around the magical powers of enslaved Africans who longed for home. Flight is a form of escape from the brutality of slavery and its debilitating legacies; it is a spiritual journey home that allows for a different kind of self-awareness rooted in a past that one now possesses. Think of Milkman in Toni

Morrison's *Song of Solomon*.[2] For him, flight is both escape and ascent. But in this story slavery and the ugliness of American racism are not mentioned. The men are already dead and in Heaven, for what reasons we do not know. The ugliness of life is assumed, ascent has happened, and what matters is the insistence on flying anyway. You must maximize your gifts no matter the costs. The wings were his, after all, and even when they were taken away, this Black man relished the life lived even in death. He was a flying fool when he had them.

Flight takes on a distinct resonance here. We still have the features of escape and ascent, implied at least, but in this folktale flying is bound up with a certain idea of the self and a way of being in the world that isn't about the past but about *the living*. Do not let people, and most of all don't let yourself, crumple your feathers.[3] I have come to see that this vision of flight shapes the view of Black democratic perfectionism I commend in these lectures. I believed then, as I do now, the wings belong to us, still.

— *Looking Back* —

The memory is a living thing—it too is in transit. But during its moment, all that is remembered joins, and lives—the old and the young, the past and the present, the living and the dead.

EUDORA WELTY

MY SOUL LOOKS BACK and wonders. The details are not hard to remember—at least some of them aren't. They haunt, and, somewhere lodged in the cracks and crevices of the memories are indications of what was to come. Past as prologue, I guess, or as prophecy.

I have avoided returning to these lectures for over a decade now. Perhaps "the troubles" of the intervening years have corrupted my attention. So much has happened since those three days at Harvard in September 2011, with friends and colleagues gathered and with Henry Louis Gates Jr., oddly enough, sitting in a big, comfortable chair next to the podium from which I spoke. I became the founding chair of the Department of African American Studies at Princeton University in 2015. I wrote four books. Each of them found their beginnings in these lectures. My son grew into a grown man. Life happened, and it has not been easy.

In between then and now, the horrors of this country and of our times (past and present) pressed in. The excitement of the Obama years waned as the bodies piled up like the images in an Alexander

Gardner Civil War photograph. Police killed Black people at an alarming rate. Americans witnessed only a fraction of it on video, but far more than we could handle. Some of the images have stayed in my head even when newer horrors nestled up beside them.[1] The Tea Party ran John Boehner and Paul Ryan out of Congress. White supremacist organizations became increasingly dangerous. They rebranded themselves as the alt-right and, like a virus, infected the body politic with a more virulent and shrewd strain of a familiar and native disease. They made themselves known in Charlottes-ville as they marched and shouted, "Jews will not replace us," and left Heather Heyer dead in the street. More deaths would follow in El Paso and in Buffalo. Fear and panic grabbed hold of the country as demographic data revealed the "browning of America," and white people—at least those who felt they could be nothing but white—clung to their gods and longed for the days when people who looked like me knew their place.

When I delivered these lectures, Trayvon Martin and Michael Brown were still alive. Breonna Taylor had just graduated from high school and was imagining what her future might look like. Eric Garner and Freddie Gray were alive. George Floyd had not moved from Houston to Minneapolis. Sandra Bland was still posting her video commentary "Sandy Speaks."[2] Patrice Cullors, Alicia Garza, and Opel Tometi had yet to post anything about Black Lives Matter. The QuikTrip gas station in Ferguson, Missouri, was still doing business, and the Penn-North CVS in West Baltimore served a community barely keeping its nose above water.

Donald Trump seethed in the shadows. President Obama's jokes about him at the Press Club in April of 2011 left Trump red-faced with a clenched-teeth grin. His rage joined with the anger of millions of white Americans and a smattering of others who believed they were losing the country. I could not have imagined then that the nation would soon elect someone so vile as its next president and that people would ransack the Capitol in his name. I was so confident white America would not elect Donald Trump that in 2016 I refused to support Hillary Clinton. I wanted a more progressive politics. Vote down-ballot and leave the presidential ballot blank, I argued in *Democracy in Black: How Race Still Enslaves the American Soul.*[3] Force the Democratic Party to address substantively the circumstances of Black America in the aftermath of the Great Recession if they wanted our vote. We are more than cattle chewing cud, I exclaimed. I believed we had an opportunity to finally break the back of Clintonism, which was a mirror image of Reaganism. I was terribly wrong.

Despite Trump losing the popular vote, the majority of white America voted for him, and all hell broke loose. For four years, I watched a mediocre confidence man give license to greed, selfishness, and hatred (a combination that has distorted much of American life since the country's birth and, especially, since the election of Ronald Reagan in 1980). A major political party morphed into an autocratic political force as its members either cowered before Trump or made explicit their own commitments that America must remain a white nation for the privileged few, with working white people as their shock troops. Once again, as is often the case when the nation confronts its contradictions, we witnessed the "tricky magic" around race, an alchemy that transforms fears and hatreds into scapegoats and eases the pain of a nation still uncertain about who and what it is.[4] The so-called racial reckoning sparked by protests around police killings waned as white grievances and fears intensified. Donald Trump was at the center of it all, but he was not the cause. This was the ugly underside of the United States. Trump simply turned the country over so that all could see the shit hidden underneath.

Ominous clouds gathered and winds blew with triple fury. I could not imagine the scale of death to come. A global pandemic shut down the world and left over a million Americans dead, and Black folk died disproportionately. I lost a close friend. He told us that if he got sick, he wouldn't make it. I attended his funeral virtually; the computer kept freezing. Grief stood still. Despite those clamoring for some semblance of normalcy (neoliberalism required that we get back to buying things), nothing would ever be the same. People disappeared. All forms of death got swallowed up in a pandemic that moved like a biblical plague. As adrienne maree brown writes, "The closer the death, the less words [could] hold it."[5]

In the middle of unimaginable loss, Americans found themselves drowning in distrust and ignorance as Trump commended the likes of hydroxychloroquine in daily news conferences that felt like a circus clown had hijacked the microphone and beckoned us all into the center ring. Not to laugh, but to fight—a kind of political battle royale for his cruel pleasure. Some Americans refused to wear masks in the name of liberty. Others traded in conspiracy theories about the virus and the potential vaccine. Amid the circus, Americans had to deal with their dead *alone.* No public rituals. No collective sorrow. People couldn't sit shiva. In New Orleans, folks could not march in a second line. No wakes. No family gathering at the bedside to say goodbye. Grief felt like the heat of a Mississippi August. Sticky. Suffocating. People *did not die right,* and, where I am from, where the Spanish moss hangs from bald cypress trees and casts dark shadows on the river water, when people don't die right, they refuse to stay in the ground. The ghosts haunt us with our memories and loneliness as their weapons.

It felt, and feels, like the very structure of our way of life broke in two. Some of us were locked away in our homes, protected by our economic status. Others, now thought of as "essential workers" yet once seen as disposable workers, were, in reality, still disposable as they faced the virus head on so that the rest of us could eat and shop. They died at a disproportionate rate, too.[6] Seasons passed. The death in autumn gave way to the chill of winter and people snapped like dry twigs. The promise of spring sat broken in the face of unimaginable grief, and the release of summer revealed how silly and selfish we were as people gathered on beaches and in bars only to spread the virus. The dead kept piling up: "A plague is no respecter of delusions."[7] Police kept killing Black folk.[8] Trump kept being Trump. The nation teetered on the edge of collapse as political divisions deepened and everyone struggled to breathe because the political air was so damn thick.

Life felt like what James Baldwin described in 1972 in *No Name in the Street:* "There really has been some radical alteration in the structure, the nature, of time." For me, it wasn't so much the sense of fragmentation Baldwin felt after the collapse of the Black freedom movement, when it was as if time and people shattered into pieces. Of course, people broke in two. I broke. (I am still trying to write my way out of the abyss to see how the world has cracked, and cracked me, wide open.) But what I felt then and what I feel now is the *compression* of time itself, as if past and present have been mushed together with details oozing out but temporally detached. Compressed or lost? No matter. The details remain amid the ruins like shattered colored bottles—bright reds, dusky greens and blues—alongside broken clay pots. Maybe this is why I have not returned to these lectures until now. The details of the past have been present all along, a mosaic of ruins shaping my work. I am reminded of Walter Benjamin's question, "Shouldn't we . . .

speak of events which affect us like an echo—once awakened by a sound that seems to have issued from somewhere in the darkness of a past life?"[9] It seems we have no choice. "All that remembers joins, and lives . . ."

In 2011, when I stepped to the podium in Cambridge, Massachusetts, I was more concerned with the effects of the Obama presidency on the form and content of Black political struggle and on how we might imagine a more democratic politics considering the temptations and sins revealed over the Obama years. While I worked on the lectures, I detailed those sins in another manuscript that I was writing, which would become *Democracy in Black*. There I sought out Black Lives Matter activists and made more explicit a Black democratic politics untethered from the custodial politics that Adolph Reed so brilliantly describes. But with these lectures, I wanted to turn our gaze away from politicians and court prophets and to mine what was possible in *us*, what was possible in *me*. Ralph Waldo Emerson and James Baldwin loomed large. John Dewey and Ella Baker, too. I wanted to bring the prophetic down to the ground, to imagine the heroic as the possession of all of us and to trace the broad outlines of a politics I call "Black democratic perfectionism," in which ordinary people, full of self-trust, see themselves, as Baker insisted they do, as the leaders they have been looking for. They would be skeptical of prophets of a certain sort who herald politicians as the fulfilment of the struggles of ordinary Black people as well as suspicious of those who claim to possess the truth and urge all of us to follow them.

I suspect now, looking back, that this particular line of inquiry was about something more than false prophets and the state of Black politics during the Obama years. It was, in part, about *me*.

And I suspect, if I am to be honest, *this* looking back is part of the ongoing work of gathering the broken pieces that I am. These lectures occasioned not only an opportunity to clarify my thinking and commitments about democracy and race in the United States, but also to imagine myself as an intellectual in a different way. I wanted to break through a certain academic shell and trust *my* voice on the page. I wanted to fly.[10]

On a certain level, I enacted the form of perfectionism I was commending. I wanted to leave behind my romance with a Black political golden age and that required more than an adolescent rejection of the "the sixties."[11] I needed a clear sense of where *I* stood in this tradition that mattered so much to me. And that understanding, disconnected from how I was raised (a Black southern child to be seen but not heard, a kind of invisibility that mirrored ironically the world on the other side of the veil), would release me to reach for something different, something higher.[12] This was the anguish of self-creation, of conjuring an original relation to a world haunted by history and by the dead who did not die right. The same held true for my intellectual inheritances: I had to get clearer in my head about my commitments and the trajectory of my intellectual projects. Self-trust was desperately needed. "Ne te quaesiveris extra," as the epigraph to Emerson's essay "Self-Reliance" commends.[13]

But this felt like the conceit of a white man. I say this not to make a crude appeal to easy race thinking, but rather to insist on the import of historical matters. To be sure, Emerson's view of the self did not deny the constraints of our inheritances. Tradition matters. Sophomoric readings of "Self-Reliance" often leave us with individuals unencumbered by the past and free to do whatever they imagine as good for them. But Emerson understood profoundly that we are born in a world not of our own making, and that we often find ourselves caught up in circumstances, in ways of acting, that do not originate with us. It is in the hard work within and against our environments that individuality takes shape. "We must have an antagonism in the tough world for all the variety of our spiritual faculties, or they will not be born," he wrote in "Man the Reformer."[14] Ralph Ellison would describe this as "antagonistic cooperation" best exemplified in the jazz quartet: that sense of individuality found and developed within and against the group.[15]

But Emerson goes a step further. He holds that the development of our best selves, the cultivation of our individual talents, may settle our obligations to others: "You may fulfill your round of duties by clearing yourself in the direct, or in the reflex way. Consider whether you have satisfied your relations to father, mother, cousin, neighbor, town, cat and dog; whether any one of these can upbraid you. But I may also neglect this reflex standard, and absolve me to myself. I have my own stern claims and perfect circle."[16] Here the command "Do not seek outside yourself" (especially in the hands of those sophomoric readers of Emerson)[17] can take on a kind of self-regard that fouls the air, and one that I cannot fully embrace given that I am bone of bone and flesh of flesh of those who bear the wounds of American slavery and racism. Selfishness amounts to a sin against the Holy Ghost. It is a quarrel with Emerson, or with a particular version of Emerson, these lectures make explicit and one that is not easily settled. But the stakes are deeply personal.

The use of autobiography, for example, reflects the lessons learned from my reading of James Baldwin. He constantly tells the story of his vexed relationship with his father, detailing the primal wound that moved him about until he took his last breath. I open the second lecture with a wound by my father (I doubt he remembers what he did) as a way of framing my own embrace of Malcolm X as a moral exemplar, of setting up my skepticism about the role of the heroic in democratic politics, and of fore-shadowing the need to balance piety, wound, and self-creation. It is a delicate balancing act, I must say, to acknowledge one's in-debtedness to others, especially to loved ones, and to admit of the bruises and cuts left by hard love. One is tempted to leave it all behind and suffer silently the anxiety of influence, declare oneself as unprecedented, and bury the dead once and for all.

But Jimmy insisted on telling and retelling the story about his father in order to possess the story for himself and to use it as raw material for self-creation. This need to possess one's story reflects an Emersonian insight colored a deep indigo blue. The past matters even as we search for our own unique voice. "We must not be sacks and stomachs," Emerson declared in *Representative Men*. We are more than mere followers or imitators, but we can't put aside, by a simple act of the will, our inheritances even as we choose our an-cestors. "I yam what I yam."[18] Baldwin put it this way in *Nobody Knows My Name:* "I still believe that the unexamined life is not worth living: and I know that self-delusion, in the service of no matter what small or lofty cause is a price no writer can afford. His subject is himself and the world and it requires every ounce of stamina he can summon to attempt to look on himself and the world as they are."[19]

In these lectures, my eyes rest on both the country and me. The past comes into view not to make us cower or to engage in sup-plication, but to give an account of the present in order to release us into being otherwise. It is a historical sense soaked in anxiety. A passage from T. S. Eliot's "Tradition and the Individual Talent" comes to mind:

> If the only form of tradition, of handing down, consisted in
> following the ways of the immediate generation before us

in a blind or timid adherence to its successes, "tradition" should positively be discouraged. We have seen many such simple currents lost in the sand; and novelty is better than repetition. Tradition is a matter of much wider significance. It cannot be inherited, and if you want it you must obtain it by great labour. It involves, in the first place, the historical sense, which we may call nearly indispensable to anyone who would continue to be a poet beyond his twenty-fifth year; and the historical sense involves a perception, not only of the pastness of the past, but of its presence.[20]

A delicate balance indeed. We cannot be concerned solely with the future as if the past is not present in our current living. If we do, hubris will hollow out our dreams. Any struggle for the world as it could be must be imagined close to the ground in the world as it is *and as it came to be.*

In 1974 I was six years old. Unbeknownst to me, as I built forts with friends in the backyard and searched for crawdads in shallow pools of water gathered in ditches, a Black man whose work would shape my life took the podium at Harvard that year. Ralph Waldo Ellison found himself in Cambridge as he addressed the Harvard class of 1949 on its twenty-fifth anniversary. He understood well the backdrop of his remarks. Black Power dominated the Black political scene. The crisis of Watergate raged. Richard Nixon would soon become the first president to resign his office. The country felt like it was coming apart at the seams. Ellison took the stage with a clear-eyed sense of the perils facing the nation. Humor framed his efforts, however. He joked about Harvard and about the fact that the university's speaking invitation was addressed to

Ralph Waldo Emerson. That humor served as a lesson of sorts: that no matter the difficulty of the hour the students mustn't take themselves too seriously even as they faced the complexity of their circumstances. It also announced his intention to think with and against Emerson, "to show forth through the ghostly lineaments of a white philosopher and poet."[21]

Ellison told the story of what happened in the summer of 1953 when he was last on Harvard's campus. He stumbled upon the wall of Memorial Hall engraved with the names of Harvard men killed in the Civil War. It was a moment of revelation: that these men had given their lives, in part, for his freedom and that he had lived his life unaware of this indebtedness. "Standing there I was ashamed of my ignorance," Ellison told the students, "and of the circumstances that had assigned these young men to the shadows of our historical knowledge."[22]

Those circumstances would draw his attention for much of the lecture. The nation had turned its back on the sacrifices of these men and had "repressed the details of the shameful abandon-ment of those goals for which they had given their lives." That betrayal of both the ideal of democracy and the memory of those who gave their lives for it haunted the country. It was a denial of the past, of history and its relevance to American life and its sig-nificance to any robust sense of American individuality and iden-tity. "A discontinuity had been imposed by the living," he said, "and their heroic gestures had been repressed along with the de-tails of the shameful abandonment of those goals for which they had given up their lives." All to maintain an American innocence in the face of "the evil which [sprung] from our good intentions."[23]

But, for Ellison, "innocence" misnames the ethical blindness often attributed to Emerson and to the nation. "Hubris" is a better word: a tragic flaw in our national character and perception accompanied by arrogance and insolence. For him, the most damaging form of insolence and pride in the drama of American society was racism, and American hubris with regard to such matters imperiled this fragile experiment in democracy. The struggles of the mid-twentieth century brought all of this to the fore, Ellison declared. The Civil War had not yet been settled. Those struggles, even in light of the intense white backlash of the Nixon era, offered the nation an opportunity to "[face] up to the reality of the Americanness of American diversity, and to the past which made us what we are." And here Ellison quotes T. S. Eliot: "*What we have inherited from the fortunate / We have taken from the defeated.*"[24] We must not forget what has made us who we are. With this insight, Ellison returns to Emerson without the arrogance and insolence of a certain reading of self-reliance: that the antidote to American hubris is "conscience and consciousness, more consciousness and more conscientiousness!"—an intelligent awareness of who we are. In his hands, Emerson crosses the proverbial railroad tracks and sings the blues.

I suppose I sought to do something similar during my time in Cambridge, although close to fifty years later it did not require the wall in Memorial Hall to stage my efforts. History mattered (and matters) in my call for a different kind of Black political subject. I will leave it to the reader to determine whether such musings get in the way or not in these lectures, but the exercise of writing, of fighting with Emerson, on the eve of a decade of Sturm und Drang helped release me into a different way of thinking, of writing, of being.

Part of this effort involved making explicit my engagement with American pragmatism, all of which began during my graduate school days at Princeton University, another idyllic place a long way from the bayous of Moss Point, Mississippi. Encountering Richard Rorty and Kenneth Burke with Jeffrey Stout, exploring African American religious history with Albert Raboteau, and reading pragmatism with Cornel West shaped how I have come to read and understand American life. In fact, during those years, West was in the last stages of completing his important book *The American Evasion of Philosophy: A Genealogy of Pragmatism,* a somewhat Whiggish intellectual history that begins with Emerson and ends with his own prophetic version of pragmatism. As West reads the tradition, American pragmatism is less a professional exercise and more so a continuous interpretation that tries to make sense of America under specific material conditions and in a particular historical moment. For him, and I share this view, pragmatism, rightly understood, is a form of cultural criticism in the face of America's uncertainty about who and what it is. It also considers the consequences that follow from the ongoing refusal of the country to know itself.

John Dewey matters here. Dewey believed that philosophy should be thought of "as a method of locating and interpreting the more serious of the conflicts that occur in life and a method of projecting ways for dealing with them: *a method of moral and political diagnosis and prognosis.*"[25] On this view, philosophy is more than a stale academic exercise concerned with technical puzzles or neat piles of distinctions. What philosophers do matters insofar as the work addresses the circumstances of our living. Dewey's historicism and his efforts, however flawed, to engage the myriad problems of his day inspired, along with Emerson's initial evasion, West's prophetic pragmatism and my own. I have spent the better part of my career trying to get clear on what this inheritance means for me as I interpret the experiences of Black people in the United States.[26] West would eventually find the label of pragmatism too limited for his own purposes and reach for other resources to engage in the kind of work he would come to call "Chekhovian criticism." Ironically, I found myself, despite the broad political concerns of these lectures, engaged in a narrow dispute with my teacher over the pragmatism that he has since left behind. Fathers cast long shadows.

I do not see this as the kind of patricidal performance that characterizes so much of Black letters, especially among Black men. I felt no need to slay the father. My love for Cornel runs too deep for that. But I had to get a better sense of where he ends and I begin. We must not be sacks and stomachs, right? Initially, my plan was to delete this section of the last lecture (especially given the expanded engagement with Sheldon Wolin) to hide my anxiety of influence. But when read as part of an act of self-creation, the engagement with West takes on an important meaning, philosophically and existentially, at least for me. So, I have decided to leave matters as they are.

My reading of pragmatism insists that human beings, fragile and fallen though we may be, must bear the responsibility of securing by *practical* means the values we most cherish. The fate of the world is in our hands after all, as Toni Morrison suggested in her Nobel lecture.[27] I read this in John Dewey, but I learned it from the people on the coast of Mississippi who lived it intimately and intensely. Dewey conceived of pragmatism as an instrument of social improvement aimed principally at expanding democratic life and broadening the ground of individual development. For him, democracy constitutes more than a body of procedures; it is "a personal way of individual life" animated by a working faith in the possibilities of our fellows.[28] If democracy is to flourish, we must cultivate democratic dispositions in which we, along with others, demonstrate in our doings a caring outlook toward others and assume the responsibility for setting forth intelligently some ideal of a collective good life. To my mind, this describes the Black freedom struggle at its best.

This view saturates these lectures as I think pragmatically about the prophetic, the heroic, and the democratic (and implicitly disagree with those who embrace Afro-pessimism). I do so, as I have always done, by forcing an encounter between pragmatism and African American life. I bring the philosophy behind the veil (and, yes, the veil still exists): thinking about Black life and politics—about history, identity, and agency—indelibly marked by the reality of living in a society committed, at once, to democracy and to white supremacy. Thinking about how that fact colors the act of self-creation for those darker souls and how it gives new meaning to W. E. B. Du Bois's cry of "two unreconciled strivings; two warring ideals in one dark body, whose dogged strength alone keeps it from being torn asunder."[29] And knowing that, no matter the darkness of the days, we have the capacity, if we only imagine it so and dare to act, to transform our world.

All this talk about Emerson and pragmatism, about self-cultivation and faith in our ability to change the world, might seem like the musings of a madman, especially against the backdrop of the last decade. But I *am* a madman, a flying fool, who refuses to resign himself to the world as it is.

In that too, I am an inheritor. When I read James Baldwin's introduction to his 1985 collection *The Price of the Ticket,* I see him trembling for his own sanity and searching the events of his life for some indication of what was happening to him and to the country as he barreled toward the grave. America had turned its back on the promise of the Black freedom movement of the mid-twentieth century. Reaganism had enshrined greed and selfishness once again as the most important values of the land. Baldwin had to come to terms with the collapse of the movement and with the loss and the dead left in its wake. "We have lived through avalanches of tokens and concessions," he said, "but white power remains white. And what it appears to surrender with one hand it obsessively clutches in the other."[30] Melancholy and mourning saturated the writing in his last days. Trauma and rage colored the ink in his pen. Forgetfulness plagued the nation. And in this essay, Baldwin charts what happened between then and the ascent of Reagan, and what was needed if the nation was to be released from the white-knuckled grip of its ghosts. Like Ellison, he calls attention to the tricky magic that keeps America from confronting its past and its sins. "The price the white American paid for his ticket was to become white—and, in the main, nothing more than that, or, as he was to insist, nothing less."[31] That alchemical transformation, which leaves behind the particulars of the Old World and requires the captivity of those darker souls, "has choked many a human being to death here."[32]

But this "looking back" entailed more than a litany of the nation's ongoing sins. Baldwin recalls the moments and the people who gave him license to imagine himself in the most expansive of terms. He details *his* inheritance: people like Beauford Delaney who told him that "not only was I not born to be a slave: I was not born to hope to become the equal of the slave-master."[33] That he *was* valued set the stage for the arduous task of self-creation and enabled him to become the writer who would speak the truth to the nation and to the world. I say this not to deny Baldwin's wounds and fears. He offers the painful details of many of those wounds. "I was to hurt a great many people by being unable to imagine that anyone could possibly be in love with an ugly boy like me," Baldwin wrote.

"To be valued is one thing, the recognition of this assessment demanding, essentially, an act of will. But love is another matter."[34]
That act of will, made possible by being loved even when it leaves
its bruises and scars, opens the door to being otherwise.

No crumpled feathers. Beauford Delaney, Marian Anderson, and
others were Baldwin's inheritance; he was "a part of their hope."

Returning to these lectures after so many years reminds me
that when we fly and when we acknowledge the wind beneath our
wings, *we become the hope this dark world desperately needs.*

1

ON PROPHECY AND
DR. MARTIN LUTHER KING JR.

An act overtly tried out is irrevocable, its consequences cannot
be blotted out. An act tried out in imagination is not final or
fatal. It is retrievable.

JOHN DEWEY, *HUMAN NATURE AND CONDUCT*

Everything now, we must assume, is in our hands; we have no
right to assume otherwise.

JAMES BALDWIN, *THE FIRE NEXT TIME*

AT THE HEART of John Dewey's philosophy lies a romantic
impulse, a vision in which the moral imagination plays a crucial
role in our efforts to become who we hope to be as we intelligently
engage a complex and perilous world.[1] Here we see the priority of
imagination over reason,[2] where intelligent action entails habits
and dispositions attuned and attentive to the details of the social
world, action animated by passionate commitment and by imagination.[3] Dewey was dissatisfied with the way philosophers characterized reason. Reason is no special faculty set apart from desire
and passion. Instead, he preferred talk of intelligence and of the
central role of imagination in our efforts to grasp our world and
to see what is possible beyond our current conditions of living. In

Democracy and Education, for example, he wrote, "Imagination is as much a normal and integral part of human activity as is muscular movement."[4] We see its role in his 1932 *Ethics* as the inferential dimension of inquiry, where he holds off Immanuel Kant's worry about the self-indulgent implications of the imagination. For Dewey, the imagination is more than a playground for epicurean delight; it enables us to reach for the fullness of the complexity of human endeavor; it is that which makes possible a measure of distance from the cultural frames that box us in in order to transform situations and to create ourselves anew.

In this chapter, I want to push a bit farther Dewey's view of moral imagination. That is, I want to think about how the prophetic as the moral imagination works as a dimension of critical intelligence—as a decision of conduct, directed toward an as yet realized present, under conditions where matters of justice are at stake.[5] Here my aim is rather ambitious. I want to recast the prophetic in light of my reading of pragmatism. In my view, the prophetic mode isn't bound up with a form of exhortation and judgment rooted in a truth that originates elsewhere. Nor is it only about measuring the failures of the present over against the moment of covenant or a past when we got it right. Instead, as I will suggest, the prophetic is that feature of critical intelligence, in the context of particular problems faced and tragedies endured, in which life as it is experienced is critically engaged in light of life as it could be. The prophetic isn't backward looking; it is prospective in its function. Making this claim will involve a close reading of Dewey and his understanding of the moral imagination. Throughout I suggest, and I am well aware that this is a strong reading, that the moral imagination, within the exercise of critical intelligence, functions much like prophecy in its romantic register. I insist that the power of prophecy rests within us, not outside of us or as the special possession of a chosen few.[6]

All of this is to lay the groundwork for some preliminary reflections on how we might reconstruct the idea of the prophetic and the heroic in African American democratic life. This effort assumes a deep-seated suspicion about the democratic character of the prophetic tradition in African American politics and involves an admittedly idiosyncratic reading of Dr. Martin Luther King Jr. as a romantic prophet. In the end, I worry about the ways a certain view of the prophetic mode distorts and disfigures democratic debate within Black political life as some assert an authority that exists apart from the demos. The underlying purpose here is to reconceive what freedom struggles can be and do, and who ought to be their principal agents.

John Dewey, Prophecy, Neoliberalism

What occasioned these reflections, beyond my general dissatisfaction with Black political elites, was an odd encounter in Dewey's corpus. I was rereading *Individualism Old and New* (1930) and was struck by its current relevance. Dewey offers a trenchant critique of an inherited view of individualism that denies the capacities of human beings to engage in intelligent action. This denial deepens individual conformity to unjust arrangements as Americans, then as now, stand by silently in the face of deepening wealth disparity and widening social misery. As Dewey would later argue in his 1936 address at the Harvard Tercentenary Conference of the Arts and Sciences, this view of individualism, "in the very act of asserting that it stood completely and loyally for the principle of individual freedom, was really engaged in justifying the activities of *a new form of concentrated power*—the economic, [a] new form, to state the matter moderately, [which] has consistently and persistently denied effective freedom to the economic[ally] underpowered and underprivileged."[7] Dewey anticipates one of the central features of neoliberalism—what the philosopher Wendy Brown describes as its political rationality.

In Brown's view, neoliberalism isn't simply "a set of economic policies; it is not only about facilitating free trade, maximizing corporate profits and challenging welfarism." The very things we associate, say, with Reaganism or Thatcherism. Rather, neoliberalism instantiates a particular way of life and governance that extends the market into the very idea of who we take ourselves to be. As Brown writes, "Neoliberalism normatively constructs and interpellates individuals as rational, calculating creatures whose moral autonomy is measured by their capacity for 'self-care'—the ability to provide for their own needs and service their own ambitions." She goes on to say that "a fully realized neo-liberal citizenry would be the opposite of public-minded, indeed it would barely exist as a public. The body politic ceases to be a body but is, rather, a group of individual entrepreneurs and consumers" in competition with themselves.[8] The result, of course, is a contraction of the idea of the public good and an anemic view of mutual obligation because selfishness and greed trump all other values.[9]

Dewey appeared to be tracking this development in its earliest phase and argued that what was needed in response to these conditions was a *reconstructed* notion of individuality consonant with the moment, in which "ideas and ideals are brought into harmony with the realities of the age in which they act."[10] With liberalism's failure, what was required was a more adequate view of individuality in light of market forces that sought to contain democratic energies. We needed to imagine ourselves and our being together differently if we were to respond effectively to the new forms of concentrated power.

This reconstructed view of individualism, Dewey maintained, would be decidedly social and seen as developing within and through interactions with our fellows and by means of enabling social structures (e.g., public schools). In the interim, forces would continue to unhinge the old individualism.

> Instances of the flux in which individuals are loosed from the ties that once gave order and support to their lives are glaring. They are indeed so glaring that they blind our eyes to the causes which produce them. Individuals are groping their way through situations which they do not direct and which do not give them direction. The beliefs and ideals that are uppermost in their consciousness are not relevant to the society in which they outwardly act and which constantly reacts upon them. Their conscious ideas and standards are inherited from an age that has passed away; their minds, as far as consciously entertained principles and methods of interpretation are concerned, are at odds with actual conditions. This profound split is the cause of distraction and bewilderment.[11]

Dewey does not specify the nature of the new idea of individuality; he does "not see how it can be described until more progress has been made in its production." Instead, he urges us to redirect our energies and to redeploy our imaginations in the service of creating a context in which a new individuality could in fact emerge and flourish.

I should say a word about the place of reconstruction in such an effort. Reconstruction characterizes an intellectual procedure that involves, among other things, refurbishing ready-at-hand terms that have lost their clarity because of the changing conditions informing their use. What is implied by the use of a word or a phrase (e.g., "individualism," "race," or "the color line") at the dawn of the twentieth century might not register the same meanings in the second decade of the twenty-first century and in the context of neoliberalism's stranglehold. Failure to attend to those differences may result in confusion and misdiagnoses. Yet unclear words still influence how we see, describe, and understand our experiences. Reconstruction, then, amounts to (1) a strong reading of the currency of particular words (in light of problems faced with intelligence), (2) an attempt to establish an original relation to their use (by exposing a bad question at the heart), and (3) an effort to open their meanings to doings and sufferings currently in view (by revealing historical nerve endings that excite the present). We see philosophers of race who aren't eliminativists (those who argue that we should rid ourselves of race talk altogether) do this with race language, for example. They offer us a way to think about the word that orients us more effectively to our current circumstances. For Dewey, "reconstruction can be nothing less than the work of developing, of forming, of producing (in the literal sense of that word) the intellectual instrumentalities which will progressively direct inquiry into the deeply and inclusively human—that is to say, moral facts—of the present scene and situation."[12] A reconstructed view of individualism, in this case, does exactly that given the way the old view of individualism denied / denies freedom by perversely claiming it.

————————————

In the face of new forms of concentrated power, Dewey called for an imaginative leap. He wanted us to perceive beyond the constraints of the moment in order to envision and enact an effective remedy to social ills. Here we can see the prophetic workings of the imagination. Dewey says as much. Near the end of chapter 4 in *Individualism*

Old and New, he writes: "There is a *prophetic* aspect to all observation; we can perceive the meaning of what exists only as we forecast the consequences it entails."[13] Anticipation of what could be is essential to our critical understanding of what is. We imagine what is possible as we decide to act in one way as opposed to another and that imagining grounds our efforts to navigate the problematic situation faced. That is the exercise of intelligence. We engage in directed operations aimed at the modification of conditions, and it involves the imagination insofar as we are able to perceive what is before us in light of what could be. To my mind, this is the pathway to a reconstructed view of the prophetic—a view shorn of its selectivity (where only some get to speak prophetically) and denied its absolute authority (that the person is speaking the word of God or some such power). Instead, the prophetic, in the very exercise of critical intelligence and the central place of the moral imagination in it, takes on a more democratic function in the lives of everyday, ordinary people. This is especially important as we navigate the ongoing catastrophes of concentrated forms of power that take the very idea of freedom as its justification and deepen individual conformity to not only unjust arrangements but to evils.

We are the prophets we have been looking for. No more waiting for rainbow signs. Our imaginations can point the way toward a better world.

"The Prophet" and Imagination

Traditional understandings of the prophet carry us into a somewhat enchanted world in which unique or gifted persons offer a glimpse of the punishment and humiliation to come in light of our current failings to keep the covenant. They dazzle us with the power of their conviction and bind us, through public exhortation, to a vision of who we ideally were and of what we have tragically become. We do not think of prophets as professionals of any sort. Theirs is a task rooted, even if reluctantly embraced (think of Moses, for example), in the immediacy of convictions held and the implications of our current doings, not in some routinized practice with its own internal standards of excellence. A guild of prophets would be odd. Prophets profess and exhort with the aim of changing minds and behavior, not with the hopes of demonstrating competence. The prophet speaks, to borrow a phrase from Matthew Arnold, with "fire and strength"[14] on behalf of someone or something—be it God, nation, or muse. Her authority does not derive from some inner source or from acquired expertise; the fact that she has been chosen has little to do with her innate talents but, instead, her authority springs from the outside—from that which carries the force to compel us, or those who would listen (most don't listen at all), to act otherwise.

Of course, this raises serious concerns for democratic life. Prophets aren't interested in being convinced that they are wrong. They are charged to dispense the truth; their modes of address are typically declarative and imperative. In their most recognizable sense, prophets are the central characters in a divinely sanctioned vocation. As Nicholas Wolterstorff puts it:

> The prophet is one who speaks in the name of God. As a consequence, those who hear the prophet speaking, when he is speaking in his prophetic capacity, are confronted with that which counts as God speaking; the utterance of God is not something a person just undertakes to do; God will "raise up" the prophet, as God raised up Moses. To be a prophet requires being deputized to speak in God's name.

> In addition, God will tell the prophet what he is to say, put-
> ting words in his mouth; the prophet does not devise the
> words by himself. The prophet is commissioned to commu-
> nicate a message from God, and God will give that message
> to the prophet.[15]

This is not a mode of speech conducive to democratic deliberation
or commensurate with the exercise of public reason (although it might
spur democratic debate). "The prophet was the individual who said
NO to his society, condemning habits and assumptions, its compla-
cency, waywardness, and syncretism."[16] For some, this passionate
way of talking is a conversation stopper.

But prophetic speech involves more than forceful declarations;
it presupposes a background of relations and agreements that
make such speech possible. In this sense, the work of the prophet
is decidedly social. Her mode of address is always preceded by
other words and is a response to practices and expressed values that
we call our own.[17] Mutuality and shared experience add force and
significance to her words. Ideally, in the prophet's company, we
come to know and feel something about ourselves and about the
arrangements within which we live: a renewed sense of connection;
a heightened feeling of disdain. In short, the prophet, as Ralph
Waldo Emerson says of great men, is "the collyrium to clear our eyes"
so that we might see the vices and follies that block the way to
substantive change and remember who we have been called to be.[18]
Prophets reconstruct our vision. And, it is in the context of *common
complaint and criticism within community* (and I am mindful that
such complaint and criticism can emanate from without—the
biblical story of Jonah comes to mind)[19] that the prophetic figure
can experience the full force of established powers, and that we,
as witnesses, attribute to them madness or courage as they continue

to enact their charge irrespective of the consequences.[20] Prophets stand, then, on the border of the heroic and the heretical—and in each instance, even if a few disagree with their words and actions, something beautiful is witnessed in their piety and in the virtue of courage exhibited in their willingness to risk everything.

———————

I am sure Dewey was quite familiar with this view of the prophet. His Congregationalist upbringing in Burlington, Vermont, guarantees as much. But his use of the word "prophetic" in *Individualism Old and New* refers to a different sense of the word—one not so much bound to the charismatic, heroic figure who by some magical gift or blessing has insight into the proper order of things. Instead, he points us in the direction of *inquiry* and its centrality to democracy.

One way of thinking about Dewey's use of "prophetic" is to highlight the word's predictive function. Just as meteorologists gather data to forecast weather patterns, organisms gather relevant data in the context of problem-solving to imagine outcomes that will affect them for weal or woe. Some of us work hard to anticipate the hailstorms in our lives; and others do the same with regard to securing happiness. We in effect run ahead of actual experience in order to foresee possible consequences. And here I am not so much referring to the efforts of prophets to persuade us, but rather to the prophetic dimensions of our *decisions of conduct.* Do I ask her to marry me or not? Should I take this job out of state or should I stay home? Can we grasp the prospects of freedom even as we suffer the brutal violence of the state? Such decisions of conduct do not require a special gift of insight or foresight or an unmediated connection with a higher source (God) that commands us to speak on his behalf. No unified view of reality is required here. We need not be fortune tellers or Max Weber's charismatic mad men. Instead, this idiosyncratic use of "prophetic" seems consonant with the scientific method Dewey commends, in which he entreats us "to attend more fully to the concrete elements entering into the situation in which [we] have to act."[21] We experiment.

This view presumes that all is not settled. Matters, especially those that move us about, need *tending to* and often require that we tinker intelligently.[22] For Dewey, experience is not a self-contained event; rather, it constitutes the field of knowledge acquisition. That is to say, our engagements with environments are experiments in varying the course of events—active attempts that test us in relation to problems we face, the outcomes of which are habits that effectively orient us, at least for moments in which the irritation of doubt is absent, to our environments. Such a view urges us to jettison the comfort of "a single, fixed, and final good" and to "transfer the weight and burden of morality to intelligence" as we grapple with the messiness of our moral lives.[23]

Prophecy's role in all of this is entailed in the exercise of the moral imagination. It helps us anticipate and clarify the path ahead in order that we may intelligently redirect, if necessary, those interactions that carry us one way or another.[24] And, it is in those moments when unanticipated forces eclipse our habitual ways of living (e.g., old notions of individualism that were once liberating now, under different material conditions, constrain individuality and thwart effective freedom) that we find ourselves in need of prophetic action: conduct reflective of efforts to imagine beyond the opacity of current conditions in order "to grasp undisclosed opportunities and to generate new ideals and ends"[25] that further human flourishing.

I am not suggesting that any decision of conduct constitutes a prophetic act. Clearly the question "Do I marry her?" is of a different sort from the question "Can I grasp the prospect of freedom in light of my current experience of unfreedom?" The difference between the two, among other things, resides in the difference in the scope and force of the questions. The latter extends beyond the immediacy of those directly involved to include considerations that touch upon the lives of others; it also entails a decision that is unavoidable and the answer to which is momentous. I could easily decide not to ask my love her hand in marriage. She may never know that I entertained the idea. But the decision to imagine freedom or not is unavoidable. The very fact that I am faced with the question reveals the complexity of my experience, and whatever I decide to do will profoundly affect the life before me.

But to say that not all decisions of conduct are prophetic is not to suggest that such decisions do not *inform* prophetic action. Each decision in which the imagination is deployed in the exercise of critical intelligence is a dramatic rehearsal—where possibilities are considered and tested—for the moment that calls us to the fore; those *intelligent* decisions habituate us in such a way that when momentous occasions arise we are all capable of acting powerfully and decisively.

I do not believe that such conduct is characteristic of only unique or special individuals. The view I am putting forward is not how we traditionally understand the Hebrew prophets. I want to democratize the prophetic: to insist that we all have the capacity to engage in prophecy insofar as we all have an occasion, in the exercise of critical intelligence, to envisage an unrealized possibility in the context of efforts to secure and expand those ideals that animate our form of life.[26] The prophetic within inquiry, then, is not about a commitment to a specific blueprint or covenant (Truth); rather it entails a commitment to imagining effective possibilities beyond the limitations experienced. As such, it becomes a key feature of democratic life. Thomas Alexander has it right when he states that imagination "is a phase of activity . . . in which possible activities are envisaged in relation to our situations, thereby amplifying the meaning of the present and creating the context from which present values may be criticized, thus liberating the course of action itself. . . . Imagination is temporally complex, an operation in the present, establishing continuity with the past, anticipating the future, so that a continuous process of activity may unfold in the most meaningful and value-rich way possible."[27] Imagination, in its prophetic form, affords us the possible distance necessary to say with "fire and strength" what is wrong with our current social arrangements and to forecast the emergence of more just arrangements.[28] It is a reflection upon limits and prospects; it can be a call to pursue idealized ends and a claim about the animating values of our form of life that may require us to risk everything in their pursuit.

In this sense, Dewey stands in the romantic tradition alongside Blake, Coleridge, Emerson, and others. In their hands, the prophet becomes the poet, and in Dewey's hands and my own, the poet is evidenced in the habits of the critical inquirer (not the private ironist, but the inquirer who sees herself in community with others working to forge a more just world for our children and theirs).[29] In the romantic register, the prophet banks her all on an ability to see beyond the authorities that shape current ways of perceiving, and she stands in relation to the past not deferentially nor as an epigone, but rather as a renewer of the grounds upon which she creates / acts *intelligently.*

The past is not seen as something linear. Indeed the novelty of a problem often demands a return to the archive to account for its emergence. In other words, the emergent requires a past to lay claim to it—in effect a history that prophesies its presence. If we identify the prophetic function with the moral imagination in the exercise of critical intelligence, then the past becomes a site for funded experiences—a treasure trove of resources—that enable us to invade the future with a bit more than luck. Its citation gives shape and contour to present imaginings as, once again, a claim is being made upon it. We are not untethered or unencumbered. We are always located somewhere and in some time shaped by previous actions. The challenge involves not being swallowed whole.

We must remember that the more significant problems we face disrupt our habitual ways of doing (the past has been interrupted) and occasion the moment of inquiry. The past returns not in the form of a nostalgia for origins (to rest forever in what Harold Bloom calls the primal scene of instruction or to condemn us to a state of adolescence in relation to a heroic time that is not our own) but comes to us in the work of citation. I am reminded of Walter Benjamin's take on Marx's discussion of revolutionary time in *The Eighteenth Brumaire:* "History is the object of a construction, whose site is not the homogeneous and empty time but time filled by the now. Thus, to Robespierre ancient Rome has a past charged with the time of the now which he blasted out of the continuum of history. The French Revolution viewed itself as Rome returned again. It cited ancient Rome the way fashion cites costumes of the past." The claim of the past (its invocation in the context of prophetic speech) is not to swallow whole an as yet realized present. Instead its voicing (our attempt to claim or redeem it) often interrupts current uses of the past in the justification of the order of things. We can tell the story of the Black freedom struggle of the mid-twentieth century, for example, to disrupt its use in the disciplining of Black political dissent or to interrupt efforts to corral Black people into the Democratic Party. In the end, prophecy isn't simply about prediction; to quote Ian Balfour's wonderful formulation, prophecy "is a call and a claim . . . , a call oriented toward a present that is not present" and a claim on a past that gives possibilities depth and meaning.[30]

With this pragmatic reconstruction of the prophetic, I am not committing Shelley's mistake of trading the deification of Reason for the deification of Imagination. Richard Rorty urged us "to think of imagination not as a faculty that generates mental images *but as the ability to change social practices.*"[31] I agree. My aim is closer to the ground. I want to democratize the prophetic; I want to rethink its function within African American intellectual history and in Black political life. A certain understanding of the prophetic, especially under the conditions of late capitalism, undermines democratic energies as too many individuals invest their capacities in and relinquish their imaginations to someone who has been "called." Black prophetic voices are all too often thought to be unique individuals (typically men) with special callings that distinguish them from the rest of us. We end up giving our power over to them and are inevitably left disappointed. It is time we put such a view aside.

―――――――――

Obviously, my thinking about pragmatism and prophecy is indebted to Cornel West's view of prophetic pragmatism in *The American Evasion of Philosophy*. In a 1992 interview, West described his view of the prophetic as "a democratic one in which, in the midst of the quotidian, the commonplace, in the midst of the messy struggle in which one's hands are dirty, that one is holding onto moral convictions and tries to convince others that they ought to be accepted even though those moral convictions can still be subject to criticism and change."[32] One can see how his pragmatic commitments shaped his understanding. Even so, for my tastes, West's prophetic pragmatism is a bit too dependent upon the model of the Hebrew prophets, not so much at the level of argument but in the way he enacts his view in public.

West understands prophetic pragmatism as a form of inquiry in the context of human efforts to preserve and expand empathy and compassion in light of those operations of power that frustrate human flourishing. His is an effort to make more explicit an encounter between the abiding faith among pragmatists in the capacities of everyday people and those structural forces that constrain and limit their ability to act in the world. As such, prophetic pragmatism consists in a series of supplements aimed at building a more robust and, by extension, more effective form of pragmatism as cultural critique. West turns to Marxism, Christianity, Foucault's genealogical approach, tragedy, Chekhovian compassion, and the African American prophetic tradition because, on his view, "a lack of something" remains at the heart of this American philosophical tradition, and the adjective "prophetic" constitutes the shorthand for each of these supplemental moves.

Supplements can distort and disfigure. So much so that in some instances the noun is no longer recognizable. In his review of *The American Evasion of Philosophy,* Rorty wrote that "the basic tension [in *American Evasion*] is between a wish to evade philosophy and a hope that philosophy will be a powerful instrument of social change. This tension can also be thought of as that between the pragmatist as professor and as prophet—the pragmatist as cleaning up rubbish left over from the past and the pragmatist as the dreamer who first glimpses the concrete outlines of a better future."[33] He goes on to say that if one assumes the professorial view of pragmatism as having some true significance, beyond our narrow professional concerns, then "the term prophetic pragmatism" will sound as odd as "charismatic trash disposal."[34] Typical Rortian humor. But the criticism actually reveals a central problem with his and West's view of Deweyan pragmatism.

Neither foregrounds the significance of inquiry in their accounts; instead, we are left with redescription (Rorty's linguistic turn that turns him away from Dewey's experimentalism) and West's prophetic bricolage (what I call his strategy of supplement). Although West describes prophetic pragmatism as a form of inquiry, he says very little, if anything, about what that might mean in its details. But if we take seriously Dewey's insistence on inquiry and its relation to democratic life, we leave behind the sort of tension Rorty identifies in West (between professor and prophet), precisely because we can locate the prophetic in the very exercise of critical intelligence. Something we all can do. With this, the Hebrew prophets become a different kind of example. Hilary Putnam describes the pragmatist in this way: "What we pragmatists have in common is the conviction that the solution to the loss of the world problem is to be found in action and not in metaphysics . . . and that democratically conducted inquiry is to be trusted in this effort, not because it is infallible, but because the way in which we will find out where and how our procedures need to be revised is through the process of inquiry itself."[35] This process of inquiry (and I will take this up in more detail in Chapter 3) involves the imagination as we grapple with what is before us in light of what could be. And, more importantly, when matters of justice are involved, inquiry becomes the occasion for the prophetic act.[36] The place of prophecy resolves itself, then, into a practical consideration of the conduct of life shared with others. How might prophecy work in the moral lives of individuals, in their efforts to make claims about the character of the whole, the consequences of conduct, the conditions of flourishing, and in their "capacity to concretely perceive the actual in light of the possible"?[37]

After all, Dewey understood democracy as a "personal way of individual life; . . . it signifies the possession and continual use of
certain attitudes, forming personal character and determining
desire and purpose in all the relations of life."[38] Democracy, in the
end, is much more than a body of laws and procedures; it entails
the kind of persons we are to be in community with others. How
might a democratized view of the prophetic work in light of this
vision, especially in the hands of a subject people for whom the
prophetic function is central to their political imaginings?

I want to think about this question in the context of a different
kind of reading of a standard prophetic voice: that of Dr. Martin
Luther King Jr. While acknowledging Dr. King's indebtedness to
Black Christianity, I want to see what a preliminary reading of his
prophetic witness in this romantic register yields. My aim in doing
so is to clear the space for a more pragmatic reading of prophecy—
one which, again, emphasizes its central role in the exercise of critical
intelligence and displaces a certain model of leadership that I believe distorts Black democratic life.[39]

Dr. Martin Luther King Jr. and the Moral Imagination

To study Martin Luther King Jr.'s life is to confront the tragic realities
of our nation's racial past and present; it is to encounter intimately
the ghosts that shadow our current practices. King's was indeed a
prophetic witness. Standard accounts of his career divide that
witness into two major periods: the first begins with the Montgomery boycott in 1955 and ends with the march from Selma to
Montgomery, Alabama, in 1965. The second period starts with the
Selma march and ends with his murder in Memphis in 1968.
Throughout his public life, which saw him grace the cover of *Time*
magazine and eventually become one of the most despised men

in the nation, King's vision was grounded in the dissenting tradition of America, a tradition of public exhortation and judgment that joined criticism of unjust arrangements with calls for moral renewal, drawing on the country's founding ideals of democracy, freedom, and equality.[40] King stands then in a rhetorical tradition, the American Jeremiad,[41] which goes all the way back to John Winthrop's famous sermon in 1630, "Modell of Christian Charity," but with a difference: his was an American Jeremiad transformed by the prophetic Black church tradition.

King's prophetic imagination was nurtured in the Black church. He was a child of preachers. His father and grandfather were not simply Baptist ministers, but ministers who saw the significance of churches to the social, economic, and political realities that affected the daily lives of Black people—what the historian Clayborne Carson calls an African American version of the social gospel.[42] Given this backdrop, King likened the struggle for civil rights as one for the soul of America. His was a moral as well as political concern, where racism and poverty were evils that threatened the so-called Redeemer Nation. His message was one of a turning back to the founding ideals of the nation—not a nostalgic longing for origins but a citation in a time of crisis of the ideals that best represent who we take ourselves to be.

Of course, he had his moments of doubt. We need only recall the poignant moment recounted in *Strength to Love* when racists threatened his family. King cried out, "I am here taking a stand for what I believe is right. But now I am afraid. I am at the end of my powers. I have nothing left. I've come to a point where I can't face it alone."[43] King stands here on the brink of despair, trying very much to hold off what W. E. B. Du Bois called the temptation of doubt, and at this moment, he hears the quiet assurance of an inner voice saying, "Stand up for righteousness, stand up for truth, and God will be at your side forever."[44]

This response registers one of the powerful dimensions of religious faith (though religious adherents have no monopoly on the idea): that faith bolsters our imaginations to see beyond the limit conditions of the actual world we inhabit. Indeed, for a Black Christian like King, God's assurance transforms his relation to the world and his relation to himself. He grasps who he is in terms of the vastness that is opened up by and through his imagination; he understands his doings as directed toward something beyond where he currently stands, and that reorients him to the moment—emboldening him, as it were, to act. *Faith, then, can be understood as a tendency toward action and imagination as its central conduit.*[45]

One clearly sees this at work in the religious tradition out of which King comes. African American slaves who converted to Christianity found themselves locked in a brutal relation of domination, and their relationship to God enabled them to see, as the scholar Charles Long noted, beyond the opacity of their own condition: they imagined the possible as they endured the absurdity of the actual.[46] They held at arm's length the reality of social death by living in relation to God and with others who suffered, relations that aren't reducible to the brutality of the slave regime even as they are constrained by them. Religious imagination occasions, then, the possibility of what Robin Kelley so brilliantly calls "freedom dreams," Black utopian imaginings that characterize so much of African American strivings.

―――――――――

In 1957, King spoke of the challenges of a new age, and here we see clearly his invocation of freedom dreams. No matter the difficulty of the hour, King knew that the foundations of American apartheid had been shaken as former slaves began to understand themselves as true agents of change and as children of God. In fact, he stated that Americans of all colors stood between two worlds—the dying old and the emerging new, and the ever-pressing nature of the present stood only as a *dramatic rehearsal* for a new world desperately trying to come into being. Drawing on Emerson, King encouraged his congregation to confront their fears, for "he has not learned the lesson of life who does not every day surmount fear."[47] King dared to imagine a better world. Imagination here is not some naïve musing. Imagination is that which allows us to spy the dim outlines of a possible future unharnessed from the problems of now; imagination enables us to muster the courage to proceed in pursuit of conditions that are not readily seen; it is the conduit for a faith that encourages and emboldens us to run ahead of the evidence—what William James described as that "readiness to act in a cause the prosperous issue of which is not certified in advance."[48] And, for King and others, that readiness to act meant a willingness to risk death.

This view of moral imagination can be thought of apart from one's relation to God. Indeed, King's prophetic insistence in 1957 (in the context of Emmett Till's murder, the independence of Ghana, the loud demands of white southerners for interposition and nullification) lends itself to a reading not so much rooted in any particular religious tradition, even as we note his obvious Christian commitments, precisely because of the overtly political—constitutional and democratic—terms with which he prophesied.[49] Reading prophecy in this way opens up how we might think of King's role as an exemplar of virtuous action and democratic energies. It also challenges the model of leadership he often exemplifies, especially in the hands of political elites who use a version of King to narrow the range of what counts as legitimate forms of Black political dissent.[50] In doing so, we turn our attention away from the glare of the so-called prophet before us to the delicate task of tending to the prophetic that lies within. On this reading, King would no longer cast such a shadow over us (or, minimally, over me)—a kind of moral giant under which we cower; instead, he exemplifies what resides in each of us: the power to unsettle the present by insisting on the open-ended character of the future.

David Bromwich offers a compelling genealogy of the phrase "moral imagination" that traces its emergence in the words of Edmund Burke and its use in the poems of Wordsworth and Shelley to its enactment in the witness of Dr. King. Bromwich powerfully emphasizes that feature of moral imagination that insists that "justice to a stranger comes to seem a more profound work of conscience than justice to a friend, neighbor, or member of my own community."[51] For him, and I believe he is right here, "the use of moral imagination is to gauge the self-deception that intervenes when in the apparent service of high-minded aims we come to describe our appetites as needs."[52] Moral imagination, in Bromwich's view (and I believe this is evident in Dewey as well), among its many features, serves as a source of resistance to self-deception: when our manners or habits of self-regard warp our conduct toward others.[53] Think about the way the concept of liberty is used among certain political actors today as justification to turn a blind eye to the needs and standing of others and to transform selfishness into a good. Moral imagination is desperately needed.

Of course, there is much more to be said here. But for my purposes, Bromwich distinguishes one of the two important dimensions of moral imagination: imagination as *an act of sympathy.* Dewey maintained in his *Ethics* that "a person entirely lacking in sympathetic response might have a keen calculating intellect, but he would have no spontaneous sense of the claims of others for satisfaction of their desires." The person would be lacking in what James Baldwin describes as love. Dewey goes on to say that "a person of narrow sympathy is of necessity a person of confined outlook upon the scene of human good. . . . To put ourselves in the place of others, to see things from the standpoint of their purposes and values, to humble . . . our own pretensions and claims till they reach the level they would assume in the eye of an impartial sympathetic observer, is the surest way to attain objectivity of moral knowledge. Sympathy is the animating mold of moral judgment."[54] This aspect of imagination, that the standing of others draws us beyond ourselves and into the orbit of the aspirations, interests, and fears of others, is necessary but not sufficient for moral judgment.

Imagination also involves our capacity to see the possibilities interwoven within the texture of the actual. It is, to echo Shelley, the chief instrument of the good. *Imagination is that feature of deliberation or inquiry that guides our attention beyond the immediately experienced so that we can take heed of those lessons of the past as well as take in those as yet realized possibilities that attend any problematic situation.* It is in this sense that moral imagination acquires its prophetic quality: that the sense of the as yet realized possibility that may indeed be realized, in contrast to the actual conditions of living, can be the basis of criticism of current social and political arrangements and, perhaps more importantly, the basis of a passionate creation of a self beyond the confines and strictures of the world we presently inhabit.[55] Not only are we imagining beyond the constraints of now as a way to address social ills, we are engaged in becoming the kinds of persons that imagined world requires. That will involve an honest confrontation with who we are—where "the particulars of self-accusation" might turn over the soil, enable a new self to grow, and occasion a transformational criticism of the world that distorts and disfigures. Bromwich puts it this way: "Some contrast between what I am and what I ought to be startles me and leads to self-discontent, which then issues in remedy or redress."[56]

In 1957, the challenges of a dawning age required recognition of a shrinking world: that globalization had produced what Dr. King called a geographical togetherness and that this togetherness very much needed a spiritual grounding where our moral and spiritual genius would make possible a beloved community. He insisted that this new age required of us a commitment to excellence and understanding—that the virtues of love, mercy, and forgiveness ought to stand at the center of our lives. A world so fallen by the tragic choices of finite creatures like ourselves and by the forms of concentrated power that, by 1957, were no longer so new called for reconciliation, King argued, but it also had need of redemption such that a beloved community could come into being, where a renewed commitment to democracy could animate new forms of being together.[57] In "Creative Democracy: The Task Before Us," Dewey wrote, "Democracy as a personal, an individual, way of life involves nothing fundamentally new. But when applied it puts a new practical meaning in old ideas. Put into effect it signifies that powerful present enemies of democracy can be successfully met only *by the creation of personal attitudes in individual human beings; that we must get over our tendency to think that its defense can be found in an any external means whatever, whether military or civil, if they are separated from individual attitudes so deep-seated as to constitute personal character.*"[58] We have to become better people. This view presumes a perfectionist strand central to Dewey's view of individuality and to his idea of democracy as an ethical way of life: that individuals, under the right conditions, can reach for higher selves that deepen democratic value. But this gets arrested when those very energies are displaced onto individuals with supposed special talent and who are "divinely called" to lead us to the promised land. We stop working on ourselves and fix our eyes upon them.

King understood that in a moment of challenge and crisis, in that darkest of hours, the dawning of a new age is only made possible by those who would imagine that new age; such imaginings would broaden our horizons, enlarge our experience, and enable us to leave older selves behind. Not those who would rest on a blessed assurance. Not those who assume that everything will be taken care of in the end. Not those who would have us believe that any action would only, in the end, deepen our suffering. King understood that any new age obliged us to work. As he said in 1957,

> I have talked about the new age which is fastly coming into being. I have talked about the fact that God is working in history to bring about this new age. There is the danger, therefore, that after hearing all of this you will go away with the impression that we can go home, sit down, and do nothing, waiting for the coming of the inevitable. You will somehow feel that this new age will roll in on the wheels of inevitability, so there is nothing to do but wait on it. If you get that impression, you are the victims of an illusion wrapped in superficiality. We must speed up the coming of the inevitable.[59]

Imagining a better world is not a passive act; it is a "readying of the self" to engage courageously and intelligently—to act prophetically—on behalf of a more just order. Such "readying" or "tending" involves practices that shape our dispositions toward others: a caring of the soul that opens us up to the wounds and joys of strangers, forging habits that enable us to be suspicious of actions that deny the dignity of our fellows; and a willingness "to be still" as a pathway to address the white noise of our current living. In short, those features that are often exemplified in the prophetic act are cultivated in our daily lives, readying us for the moment(s) in which courage and risk are needed. (I am reminded of a conversation with the late Bob Moses, the brilliant organizer of the Student Non-violent Coordinating Committee [SNCC]. He talked about an ethic of caring within SNCC: that each member decided to hold him or herself accountable to the responsibility of tending to people who were invisible to the larger society, of tending in such a way that they—poor, Black sharecroppers—could become who they were capable of being.)

Yet, the relative success of the movement, the eventual passage of the Civil Rights Act of 1964 and the Voting Rights Act of 1965, accentuated for King as he grew older "what . . . needed to be done before the poor, the powerless, and the racially disadvantaged could begin to achieve equality."[60] As he looked out he saw, despite the accomplishments of the movement, a country still at war with its ideals, with itself. Watts exploded in 1965 and urban uprisings consumed the nation for the next three years; the Vietnam War divided America, and his own opposition to the war shattered traditional civil rights coalitions. In a speech delivered on March 16, 1968, King put the point succinctly: "I must honestly confess that I go through moments of disappointment when I have to recognize that there aren't enough white persons in our country who are willing to cherish democratic principles over privilege." King increasingly was aware of the fact that America was on the verge of destruction and felt more strongly than ever a prophetic duty to warn the country against its hubris.

The price of change up to this moment had been cheap, King warned, for it cost very little and required no redistribution of wealth to desegregate the South. But the sickness of the nation's soul required much more: it necessitated structural change. King continued to believe that the spirit of democracy would overcome the evil of racism and economic exploitation. But a genuine transformation had to occur: America had to be born again. As he wrote in *Where Do We Go from Here?*, "We must honestly admit that capitalism has often left a gulf between superfluous wealth and abject poverty, has created conditions permitting necessities to be taken from the many to give luxuries to the few, and has encouraged smallhearted men to become cold and conscienceless so that, like Dives before Lazarus, they are unmoved by suffering, poverty-stricken humanity."[61] As Dewey identified in *Individualism Old and New* in 1930, King recognized the forces that sought to deny effective freedom to the vast majority of the world, and he called for a fundamental reordering of our values and a refashioning of the selves who would live them.

In his last Sunday sermon, on March 31, 1968, at the National Cathedral in Washington, DC, King took as his text a passage from the book of Revelation: "Behold I make all things new, former things are passed away."[62] As he stood on death's doorstep, his imagination worked to see beyond the moment. King understood that some of us were sleepwalking, and he offered a lesson in "remaining awake through a great revolution."[63] Much work needed to be done. He understood the depth and breadth of the evil faced. Racism, poverty, and militarism threatened the soul of the nation.

King's prophetic voice called us to attention, and he offered us, through his words and deeds, an opportunity to imagine for ourselves a more just and loving world. We had to become better people. King's words and witness urged us to see ourselves, as Bromwich and Dewey would have us do, "as both doer and object, who asks what a given act is doing to himself and his neighbors" and in doing so we become "less prey to an imagination heated by proselytism and war."[64] A self-critical disposition, not a self-righteous one, was needed if the country was to be born again. King exemplified the claim, in his sacrifice, that democracy is a way of life predicated on a working faith in the possibilities of who we can become. But this was not a naïve faith. On April 4, 1968, King lay dead on the balcony of the Lorraine Motel from an assassin's bullet. That working faith is, and has always been, blues-soaked.

None of what I have said dismisses the depth of King's religious convictions and how those convictions set his imagination on fire. Religious certainty about the future animated much of King's public ministry even as he urged Americans to become co-participants in that future's realization. Jesus on the cross mattered to him. But I have sought to disentangle the prophetic function from the certainty of King's religious worldview and, in doing so, to bring him back down to us. I want him to be a different kind of exemplar. I want to scale down our utopian musings so that we may see them as idealizations that spur us to act without evidence of guaranteed success, where the spell of chosen people with the Truth in their hands is finally broken. No more prophets descending from mountaintops. Rather, I want to bear witness to the multitudes of prophetic acts by ordinary people striking the blow for freedom in the face of a world that insists we all become like sacks and stomachs in need of heroes to liberate us.

2

ON HEROISM AND MALCOLM X

No man, in all the procession of famous men, is reason or illumination, or that essence we were looking for; but is an exhibition, in some quarter, of new possibilities.

RALPH WALDO EMERSON, "USES OF GREAT MEN"

It takes strength to remember, it takes another kind of strength to forget, it takes a hero to do both.

JAMES BALDWIN, *GIOVANNI'S ROOM*

A Beginning

"What are you, a fag or something?" my father asked. He said it with a look that always frightened me. His arms, with open hands, would hang at his side; the weight would shift to his right foot; his head would tilt slightly and with squinched eyes he would stare. I would freeze. My uncle, who has long since lost his memories, leaned forward on the couch with a wry smile as he awaited my answer. Something cruel was transpiring—a ritual that, I suspect, both of them lived through as a child and now relished repeating from the other side. "I was playing with Angel," I said, trying to hold back the tears, for if I started to cry, like I did most times, it, whatever "it" happened to be at the moment, would only get worse. In other situations, my older brother would tell me to stop crying, that I shouldn't look him in the eye when he yells. I never learned. I always looked him in his eyes. I always cried.

Angel was a beautiful and precocious fifth grader in our neighborhood. I laid an elaborate plan to garner her attention through an intense game of hopscotch. She drew the hopscotch pattern on the street. Eight sections with exquisitely drawn numbers. She tossed her rock, lifted her left leg, hopped over square one, and then continued flawlessly to square eight—only stepping down with both legs on three and four—turned around, hopped back to square two, picked up her stone, hopped in square one, and then out. She threw her hand on her hip, flashed her rock and a smile. My intention was to fail miserably at this. I would step on every line, lose my balance repeatedly, and ask her to show me how to do it again and again. And then came the scream. "Get your ass down here!" my dad yelled from the yard. Startled, Angel looked at me. I ran home, and there I was in the foyer of my father's house—humiliated with a question about *my* manhood.

Broken relationships between African American men and their fathers can seem cliché these days. We are wounded, the story goes, and the source of our pain, more often than not, rests with our battered relationships, if they exist at all, with our fathers. President Obama's 2009 address at Apostolic Church of God in Chicago traded on this commonsensical view as he demanded absent dads step up to their responsibilities. "We need fathers," he noted, "to realize that responsibility does not end at conception. We need them to realize that what makes you a man is not the ability to have a child—it's the courage to raise one." Such chastisements are quite familiar in Black communities, especially in the pulpits of Black churches. What gave these words their power on this occasion—and indeed each word worked like a magical talisman—was that they were uttered by the first African American president, confirming what white America thought it already knew and what we were now forced to admit (even if we knew it wasn't quite true).

I invoke an autobiographical moment not to join the rather tiresome chorus of voices about failed dads. Mine is not Barack Obama's concern (especially since I believe his Chicago address was a crass political move). I have come to know, however difficult the journey, that my father loved me in the only way he knew how. He was, and remains, the most responsible man I know. My father delivered mail in the Mississippi heat for thirty-four years. At the age of twenty-one, he married my mother (she was twenty). They had four children at a very young age. Basically they grew up with us. Despite the challenges, he kept a roof over our heads and food on the table. And he tried to prepare me and my siblings for a world that he believed posed an immediate danger to us. He used to say, "If you can survive me, not much in this world can shake you."

My purpose in telling the story is much like that of James Baldwin. Baldwin insisted on retelling the story of his primordial wound: a father who failed to love him because the world—a world organized without him in mind—defeated him daily. That defeat and the rage that inevitably followed spilled over, drowning some, but touching all within its reach: "Between his merciless children, who were terrified of him, the pregnancies, the births, the rats, the murders on Lenox Avenue, the whores who lived downstairs, his job on Long Island—to which he went every morning, wearing a Derby or a Homburg, in a black suit, white shirt, dark tie, looking like the preacher he was, and his black lunchbox in his hand—and his unreciprocated love for the Great God almighty, it is no wonder our father went mad."[1] Over his lifetime, Baldwin revisited the story of his father, with varying detail and less judgment, because it was his way of possessing the wound for himself. Indeed, the daunting task of self-creation for him, and for me, required and requires a never-ending struggle with such wounds, *with the past*, in order that we may be released into new possibilities. Baldwin wrote in 1965:

> History, as nearly no one seems to know, is not merely something to be read. And it does not refer merely, or even principally, to the past. On the contrary, the great force of history comes from the fact that we carry it within us, are unconsciously controlled by it in many ways, and history is literally present in all that we do. It could scarcely be otherwise, since it is to history that we owe our frames of reference, our identities, and our aspirations. And it is with great pain and terror that one begins to realize this. In great pain and terror one begins to assess the history which has placed one where one is, and formed one's point of view. In great pain and terror because, thereafter, one enters into battle with that historical creation, Oneself, and attempts to re-create oneself according to a principle more humane and more liberating.[2]

In my case the effort at self-creation has involved navigating the overwhelming, and sometimes overbearing, presence of my father *and* negotiating a nostalgic longing for a political moment that by accident of birth I could (and can) never possess. For whatever reason, I have always felt born out of time and place. It is an anxiety of influence of sorts—of being born too late, of living in the shadows of what has already been done and said. Think about it. I was born in 1968, a few months after Dr. Martin Luther

King Jr.'s assassination and in the middle of a nation on fire. All the cultural markers of significance of my young adult life, the events and images that captured my imagination, pointed to the Black freedom struggles of the 1960s and 1970s. The elegance of Dr. King, the rage of Malcolm X, the style of the Black Panthers, and the courage of Ella Baker represented a moment that required heroes. But what was left in my hands? How might I imagine myself in light of the greatest generation America has ever produced? It is precisely in this convergence of a need for my father's love and my romance with "the sixties" that the task of self-fashioning was lost in the fog of an imagination under siege.

My primal scene of instruction consisted in a wound inflicted by a father who failed to love appropriately and in an often paralyzing sense of belatedness that made me, at times, a sycophant to the supposed grandness of our past. This scene, in all its messiness, combined with the lived experiences of being an African American man coming of age in the Reagan years, casts in relief what Stanley Cavell calls "Emersonian perfectionism." For Emerson, each of us is tasked to ascend to higher forms of excellence, to a higher sense of ourselves, which requires the abandonment of older versions of who we take ourselves to be. Jeffrey Stout puts it best: "The higher self congeals out of the highest intimations of excellence you can intuit from where you stand. Excellence and sacred value are the kinds of goodness that matter most for living well."[3] The daunting challenge of seeking a higher self in a world that denies one standing because of the color of one's skin is bad enough. But to seek that self in the shadows of those who heroically resisted those practices to make *you* possible and to do so amid the wounds of a personal life lived, where love left its bruises, gives added meaning to W. E. B. Du Bois's cry of "two unreconciled strivings."[4]

The self to which I refer is not some static idea that exists apart from the actual life that I claim as my own. It stands not as a fixed goal the achievement of which constitutes a final resting place from the hard work of forging a unique self. Rather, the process of self-creation as I understand it refers to the effort to acquire a self, to become someone distinctive in relation to others and in light of a past that settles the ground beneath one's feet. All of which occurs, and this I know, under the conditions of late capitalism where the very idea of self-creation and self-care have been co-opted by neo-liberalism's insistence on selfishness as virtue and narcissism as standard practice.

Cavell's formulations of the next self direct us to a loftier / higher form of excellence that awaits; and it is in my striving, to echo Du Bois again, that I break free from the hold of established habits that settle me in where I now stand, and ascend—ideally to a higher self and into higher forms of excellence. The difficulty, and it is one not so easily avoided, rests in evading the fate of so many: to languish or rot in the expectations of others; to conform to the way things simply, or not so simply, are; or to fail to trust yourself because you have been dirtied on the inside so bad that "you forgot who you were and couldn't think it up."[5] Too often, the next self is blocked from view by the reality of a life lived thus far, and by the heroes we cling to as surrogates for our wounded selves.

In this chapter I want to step into the space I cleared in Chapter 1. There I insisted on the power of a certain view of individuality, one not captured by the political rationality of neoliberalism; instead, I gestured, admittedly in a romantic register, at an idea of Black individuality opened to the prophetic function that is, potentially at least, the possession of us all. I ended with an Emersonian flourish: that we must not be like "sacks and stomachs," repositories for the grand thinking and doing of others who claim to be prophets; rather we must be self-reliant change agents for our own times.

The reference to Emerson comes from his introduction to *Representative Men* (1850) and it frames what I aim to achieve. I want to think about the currency of the heroic for *our* moment. How might its invocation, in the right register, aid the emergence of a robust form of Black individuality that is at once appropriately pious toward tradition and irreverently keyed to an open-ended future? But this question requires, in my view, a prior step: that I interrogate how a particular idea of the heroic blocks my own self-imagining; how the very idea of Malcolm X, a surrogate father I found in the *Autobiography,* threatened to swallow me whole. The argument develops over the course of three sections. First, I take up the effects of a Carlylean understanding of the hero through an engagement with Barry Schwartz's provocative description of our current moment as a post-heroic age. I then turn to a reading of Emerson's *Representative Men* (shadowed by its African American revision) as a corrective to that view and as a frame for my own engagement with Malcolm X. The last section briefly takes up the *Autobiography* and the late Manning Marable's biography of Malcolm. My aim is to offer a reading of both that disrupts the admiration and delight that has often degenerated into idolatry, and to offer Malcolm X's biography as a spur to surpass his witness, as a stairway to a higher form of excellence. The aim is to take my democratized view of the prophetic and yoke it to an idea of the heroic that is within the reach of each of us.

As a young boy, growing up on the coast of Mississippi, my heroes helped me imagine a world beyond my immediate circumstances. I could not see myself trudging to the shipyard or to the paper mill like most of the adults in my little southern town, or delivering mail as my father did. Like Baldwin, the post office was *not* for me. And I was a bit too delicate to consider the armed services. Instead, my imagination opened up possibilities that everything in my actual life suggested were not within reach. My heroes typically leapt from the pages of the books I was reading. Wizards and elves stood alongside Thor and Spiderman. They displayed remarkable courage and wisdom. All had moral clarity, for their worlds were the stuff of melodrama. Evil was readily seen, and good always won the day. Against the expansiveness of such a world and the characters that inhabited it, Moss Point and its sleepy-eyed residents grew smaller, and I longed for something or someone bigger.

What I remember most about home were the silences, the unspoken words that screamed that something was not quite right. The space between people who loved hard but didn't say much about themselves or about the world that shaped them. Mystery and wound mingled. Children had to make do with the storm of emotions that came with it all. I did. I think this is something the poet Natasha Trethewey captures in this section of a poem from her collection *Native Guard*:

1865

These are things which must be accounted for:
slaughter under the white flag of surrender—
black massacre at Fort Pillow; our new name,
the Corps d'Afrique—words that take the native
from our claim; mossbacks and freedmen—exiles
in their own homeland; the diseased, the maimed,
every lost limb, and what remains: phantom

ache, memory haunting an empty sleeve;
the hog-eaten at Gettysburg, unmarked
in their graves; all the dead letters, unanswered;
untold stories of those that time will render
mute. Beneath battlefields, green again,
the dead molder—a scaffolding of bone
we tread upon, forgetting. Truth be told.[6]

W. Ralph Eubanks gets it right when he says to find a good Mississippi story, "explore the silences, for it is within the parts of our history we have chosen to shroud in silence in which our best stories reside."[7] Of course, pain and beauty are deeply entangled there, like coiled snakes in a mating ball.

It is here that my commonsensical idea of the hero was born. That person who in appearance seemed like the rest of us carried within himself something that stretched beyond our ordinary capacity; he was gifted to stand out and to stand above, and our orientation toward him was that of gratitude and longing. The hero had come to represent an archetype of the human endeavor, which exemplified an exacting mode of living, evidenced in the very way he lived a life in the face of ongoing peril.[8] He faced the firedrake. That life speaks to us—drawing us out of the narrowness of our immediate concern into an orbit of questing and challenge that cuts across time and makes possible a higher way of being and conducting ourselves.

I have in mind Thomas Carlyle's account of the heroic figure mashed together with my pre-adolescent sublime. Carlyle understands the hero in masculinist terms. The hero is that man who exemplifies in his doing an intensity of sincerity that compels him to grapple with the seriousness of things and compels us to hero-worship: "He looks through the show of things into things." All heroes, across time, exhibit this trait in their characters; they devote themselves to a relentless pursuit of truth and share this, in light of the immensity of who they are, with the rest of the world. As Carlyle writes, "All sorts of Heroes are intrinsically of the same material; that given a great soul, open to the Divine Significance of Life, then there is a man fit to speak of this, to sing of this, to fight and work for this, in a great, victorious, enduring manner; there is given a Hero—the outward shape of whom will depend on the time and the environment he finds himself in."[9] Heroic personalities are reflections of the moment that occasion their emergence; they possess a sincerity that has "in very truth something divine." And when thought of collectively, given the trials of an age, that generation—a heroic generation—provides the frames of reference for moral and practical judgment for succeeding generations.[10]

As I grew older I left behind the heroes of my fantasies. Dr. King and Malcolm X, Stokely Carmichael and Huey Newton stood in their stead. All served, I suppose, as proxies for an ideal of masculinity compromised by the lingering wounds of a father's love. Theirs was a heroic age—a time when individuals-in-community emerged from the shadows of American apartheid to challenge long-standing social customs, to upend racist laws, and to face down the brutal violence that sustained both. It was a period in which young people of all colors asserted themselves throughout the country, shattering received understandings of "masters and their so-called subordinates," and leaving the shards beneath the country's feet.

For some, the upheaval / chaos of the 1960s marked the end of heroism. Sociologist Barry Schwartz argues in *Abraham Lincoln in the Post-Heroic Era* that "as the lives of the great [were] cynically scrutinized for cruelty, treachery, prejudice, and egoism, the growth of racial, religious, and ethnic justice, real equality of opportunity, compassion, and the recognition of minority achievement and dignity expand[ed]." But this expansion carried with it the diminishing value of heroic narratives. "Excessive focus on pathology and moral shortcomings," Schwartz argues, made us all susceptible to the slave morality that so worried Friedrich Nietzsche.[11] Goods more consonant with multicultural ideals replaced strength and virility, and we became, to shamelessly steal from James Baldwin, like our bread: tasteless foam rubber. Such leveling banished any substantive ideal of greatness. We were left, Schwartz maintains, with "no feeling of having descended from a higher state of political morality, no nostalgic yearning for a sublime period in which great men walked the earth, no belief in, let alone effort to restore, earlier periods of epic heroism."[12]

This lamentation informs the cultural wars that periodically engulf the country. Just as it was for Alan Bloom and his provocative book *The Closing of the American Mind* close to forty years ago, attention to the contradictions of our society and efforts to live into a more genuinely multiracial democracy threaten the loss of a cherished way of life and, for Schwartz, that loss includes the banishment of true heroes.

But this view seems entirely foreign to me, because the men and women of the 1960s and 1970s are the giants stalking around my political imagination. Fannie Lou Hamer's testimony before the Credentials Committee at the 1964 Democratic National Convention powerfully represented the conditions of millions. It was nothing short of heroic. "If the Freedom Democratic Party is not seated now," she famously said, "I question America, is this America the land of the free and the home of the brave where we have to sleep with our telephones off of the hooks because our lives be threatened daily because we want to live as decent human beings in America?" Her willingness to risk her life to challenge Jim Crow joined with countless others who sacrificed to make real the promises of American democracy (and, given the fact that much of this work emanated from my home state of Mississippi, her actions along with Bob Moses and Amzie Moore and a host of others made *me* possible).

To my mind, this doesn't constitute the end of heroism nor does it locate heroic action in some narrow group identity politics. Despite Schwartz's inability to see this or his refusal to acknowledge it, theirs was an epic struggle in which extraordinary effort on behalf of generations to come transformed the very nature of American society and provided the frame for future self-understanding. Generations to follow would claim them as heroic defenders of a higher state of morality; grieve their passing; yearn for the moment in which each walked the earth; and constantly refer to their efforts as we seek to approximate their heroic example. Our task has been, consciously or not, to preserve and consolidate their victories. Emerson comes to mind here: "Our age is retrospective," he wrote in *Nature* (1836). "It builds the sepulchers of the fathers. It writes biographies, histories, and criticism. The foregoing generations beheld God and nature face to face; we, through their eyes."[13]

For Schwartz, following the historian George Forgie, preservation and consolidation are the telltale signs of a post-heroic moment. Forgie, for example, describes the anxieties and ambivalences suffered by the generation born after the American Revolution. Unable to fight in the war, but still close enough to the event to hear stories and to experience it as living memory, antebellum Americans sublimated their sense of belatedness by preserving and remembering the heroic deeds of the Revolutionary era, an era that placed a certain form of heroism beyond the reach of those who were its immediate beneficiaries.[14] One can readily see the parallels

with a generation of African Americans born too late to participate in the Black freedom struggles of the 1960s and 1970s but still
close enough to the moment for it to cast an enormous shadow
over their doings and sufferings. We find ourselves constantly
navigating its demand and purchase on us; ours, it would seem, is
a post-heroic generation.

I am not so convinced. Such moments simply mark the conditions of possibility for the emergence of new forms of greatness.
Fraught though the times may be, defined by a profound and
sometimes paralyzing anxiety, different and conceivably more
powerful selves may emerge on the horizon. What gets in the way
is the very idea of the hero, of the past within which she acted, and
our orientation to both.

Black Moralism and the Problem of the Hero

In Chapter 1, I put forward a view of prophecy rooted in the exercise of critical intelligence, where the moral imagination enables
us—any of us—to see beyond the opacity of now to envision an as
yet unrealized possibility. My aim was to decenter the idea of the
prophet as some extraordinary individual empowered by the certainty of his claims and sanctioned by some authority that exists
apart from us. I sought instead to democratize the prophetic
function and to locate it in our imaginative efforts to address
problems intelligently, especially when matters of justice arise.
Of course, the implicit and explicit object of my pragmatic
reconstruction was a certain idea of prophetic leadership in African American political life, an idea that undergirds, I believe, a
problematic custodial politics in which we cede our roles in Black
public life to leaders who represent us to others. In short, I worried that the idea of the prophetic within Black politics actually

undermined Black democratic life, and I turned my attention to one of my heroes, Dr. Martin Luther King Jr., to read him in a romantic register such that his legacy would call us, would call me, to a higher self instead of to a posture of supplication.

But all too often invocations of the Black freedom struggle and its heroes in the context of political argument require appropriate deference, or one risks racial impiety. This illustrates, more than anything, how the work of preserving and consolidating that Schwartz alludes to reflects a more complex devolution of the moral claims of any struggle to a kind of moralism that inverts that struggle's more radical thrust. The codification of moral claims and the routinization of methods along with increasing legitimization transform, potentially at least, passion and vision into rancor and conservation. We may find ourselves invoking rote phrases and empty slogans as well as engaging in unimaginative marches (e.g., a movement from King to Sharpton, from Malcolm to Farrakhan). The stories of "the Movement" may become justification for a disciplinary practice, as when Black voters were told "to get in line" in support of President Obama, regardless of his policies, because that support exemplified an act of piety. Perhaps we find that the very idea of blackness goes imperial, absorbing all other facets of our complex lives; or, we may hear the invocation of one of the movement's heroes as a basis for the condemnation of current practice (e.g., when former congressman Alan West stated that Dr. King would condemn the Occupy Wall Street movement or when former Atlanta mayor, Kasim Reed, in response to Black Lives Matter protests, said that "Dr. King would never take a freeway").

The authority of Black moralism rests in the temporal trace of a heroic age. Those who embrace it invoke the movement's martyrs and their achievements along with its vocabularies as a way to claim their legitimacy in the face of the eroding conditions of much of contemporary Black life. Dogmatic embrace and self-righteous certainty replace experimentation and open-ended inquiry. As such, the moralism of these confidence men (and women) actually reflects the evisceration of the sustaining moral vision of the Black freedom struggle. One consequence of this evisceration is "a kind of moralizing against history in the form of condemning particular events or utterances [read Black Power] and personifying history in individuals [read Dr. King]."[15] More explicitly, moralism in Black politics invokes history as a way of arresting politics: invocations of "the Movement" work to freeze us in the options "it" makes available (often drowning those of us who take it seriously in nostalgic longings for origins) and to tether us to the people and their surrogates (or those who claim to be them) we are expected to follow. Black moralists often deploy heroes to shut down any possibility of speaking back to tradition and of engaging in imaginative inquiry by narrowing the range of words and deeds available to us. Our posture becomes one of supplication and veneration.

The worry here is not so much the eclipse of a heroic time: that the hero is no longer possible. Rather, the problem resides in the sociopolitical and cultural context that actively works to block the way for expressions of the heroic under present conditions—conditions that, to paraphrase Nietzsche, transform our "instinct for freedom" into something that vents its energy upon itself.[16] The challenge facing individuals and generations born in the shadows of a great time involves, among other things, finding that right relation (and here I am talking to myself) between piety, wound, and self-creation.

Mine is not a concern about the consequences of leveling. Schwartz is right to hold the view that the value that affirms the dignity and standing of all people eclipses the value placed in so-called superior men standing over and above inferior men and women. But for him this becomes an ironic feature of his post-heroic age: that its signaled achievement, "the recognition of every citizen's worthiness and his inclusion into the social mainstream," marks the death of the hero. As he laments the decline of President Lincoln's stature, Schwartz writes: "Every scholar and commentator who has ever written about historical reputation asserts that the hero inspires because he embodies his society's ideals. But what if the function of the representative hero is to symbolize the equality of all men? What if the American people see in Lincoln the tendency toward the elimination rather than cultivation of distinction? In that case, Abraham Lincoln's prestige is undermined rather than reinforced by the very ideal he represents. Such is the fate of all great men in the post-heroic era."[17] I can't help but wonder what Schwartz thinks of Frederick Douglass's address "Oration in Memory of Abraham Lincoln," given at the unveiling of the Freedman's Monument in Lincoln Park, Washington, DC, on April 14, 1876. I was struck by one particularly powerful moment:

> It must be admitted, truth compels me to admit, even here in the presence of the monument erected in his memory, Abraham Lincoln was not, in the fullest sense of the word, either our man or our model. In his interests, in his associations, in his habits of thought, and in his prejudices, he was a white man. He was preeminently the white man's President, entirely devoted to the welfare of white men. . . . First, midst, and last, you and yours were the objects of his deepest affection and his most earnest solicitude. You are the children of Abraham Lincoln. We are at best his step-children; children by adoption, children by forces of circumstances and necessity.

From the beginning, Lincoln was a complicated hero.

In the end, one can't help noticing Schwartz's reluctant embrace of the expansion of democratic principles.[18] The moral flowering of the nation, for him, requires us to leave the hero behind. This idea fails to register the heroic actions of those residing on the underside of American life; instead, their actions become the occasion to bury the idea altogether. But, on my view, the Black freedom struggle of the 1960s and 1970s is an exemplification of the heroic aligned with American democratic life, and the challenge is: *How do subsequent generations step from under its moralizing shadow?* How do they find their own voice and stand in unique relation to a tradition that calls them to a higher self and to a more exacting mode of living? Here we need to think more carefully about the relation of the hero to democracy; perhaps we need to read Emerson more closely to see how the heroic as representative reflects a democratic sensibility.

Emerson, the Hero, and Representativeness

Emerson held a different view of the hero from Carlyle's. His wasn't the warrior or strong man who redirects the course of history, but the self-reliant individual mindful of the pitfalls of conformity. In *Representative Men* Emerson turned to the lives of great men as resources for the art of living, not as towering heroic figures to be worshipped or idolized. He went as far as to declare: "There are no common men. All men are at last of a size, and true art is only possible on the conviction that every talent has its apotheosis somewhere."[19] Of course, this does not deny the obvious fact of the unequal distribution of talent. Few of us exhibit the skill and imagination of Malcolm X or Ella Baker. But Emerson sets out to square that fact with the democratic value of the equality of persons.

The task in *Representative Men* was not to make us feel dwarfed by the likes of Plato, Shakespeare, and Goethe. The point was not that Carlyle's or Nietzsche's common folk are meant to be governed by strong and resolute men. Rather, Emerson sought to democratize greatness—to invoke the example of heroes who exemplify what we are *all* in fact capable of. In the end, encounters with great people serve to educate us in greatness such that we might exemplify that quality, in our own unique way, in our lives. Hero-worship blocks the way to such a realization.

Emerson understood the seduction of heroic figures, their allure and dangers. He not only explored the distinctive qualities of his exemplars; he also confronted fully their shortcomings: Plato left us with no system; Shakespeare lacked an interest in originality; and Goethe was "entirely at home and happy in his century and the world."[20] Emerson knew that great men and women enable us to see matters more clearly, but they can also, in the excess of their influence, blind us to our own excellences. As he wrote, "The attractions of greatness warp us from our place. We become underlings and intellectual suicides."[21] The epigraph to this chapter puts it bluntly, "No man, in all the procession of famous men, is reason or illumination, or that essence we were looking for; but is an exhibition, in some quarter, of new possibilities."[22] In other words, *great people exist that there may be even greater men and women to follow.* "Representativeness" becomes the operative word here, not Carlyle's "hero."[23]

The hero stands in an uneasy relation to democratic life. The gravitational pull of his personality causes us to bulge out in the direction of him, losing sight of our capacities as the certainty of the hero's position becomes our own. In light of this, Sidney Hook argued in *The Hero in History* that democracies should be deeply suspicious of heroes because the very temperament that sets heroes apart ultimately threatens the fabric of democratic life. Not that heroes *always* stand on the verge of becoming tyrants, individuals willing to rush pass the consent of others to the conclusion evident to their own sense of things. Instead, the sincerity of the hero's vision and his willingness to stand in our stead encourage the abdication of the responsibilities democracies demand. We become all too willing to give ourselves over to the hero in our midst.

To be sure, crises often require heroes, but their actions aren't necessarily mindful of the constraints of democratic life. I am thinking of Carlyle's description of the hero, not as a conqueror, but as "untamed Thought, great, giantlike, enormous;—to be tamed in due time into the compact greatness, not giantlike, but godlike and stronger than gianthood, of the Shakespeares, the Goethes!—Spiritually as well as bodily these men are our progenitors."[24] Such a view can easily slip into a form of tyranny. Democracies must transform the heroic and recast its function in light of a view of democratic virtue. As Hook notes, echoing Emerson, "A democracy should encourage the belief that all are called and all may be chosen"—that all have the potential to attain a kind of heroic stature and that the regulative ideal animating our form of life should be "every person . . . a hero."[25] This is indeed leveling; but, as Hook writes, it is a leveling up: "It is the task of a democratic society to break down the invidious distinctions in current linguistic usage between the hero and the masses or the average man. This can be accomplished in part by reinterpreting the meaning of the word hero, and by recognizing that 'heroes' can be made by fitting social opportunities more skillfully to specific talents."[26] This reconstructed idea of the hero becomes all the more difficult to instantiate when hero-worship dwarfs our self-conception, and we fail to see ourselves, rather than oligarchs and demagogues, as representative figures for our age.[27] Instead, we reach for the hem of the garment of our heroes, desperately trying to approximate *their* magical powers (while knowing we cannot) in *our* own time. To my mind, this is not the malaise of a post-heroic moment; it is, in a way, the burden of history shadowed by the distorting effects of capital.

Emerson's response to history's hold is to take possession of it by rereading its characters and events in light of individual experience. For him, "The dead sleep in the moonless night; my business is with the living."[28] But for those of us born under the bad sign of slavery's legacy, the past speaks more forcefully. Slavery's afterlife and that of Jim Crow shape much of our living and certainly frame how we might imagine ourselves in relation to a society saturated with assumptions about who we are and what we are capable of—assumptions that some would argue make the entire way of life in the West possible. In this light, the business of living requires coming to terms with the dead—precisely because their ghosts continually haunt us.

Across the proverbial railroad tracks, the temporal trace of Emerson's idea of representativeness can be found in the familiar trope of the "Race Man," or in Ralph Ellison's incantation of the "Renaissance Man."[29] Both are ideal types that function within a landscape where the life chances of African Americans are decidedly circumscribed. Both reflect, as Hazel Carby has demonstrated, an ideology of masculinity that often overdetermines how we conceive of Black leadership, how we engage in Black politics, and how we take up the task of self-creation. But each inflects the idea of representativeness in different ways.

In *Black Metropolis* (1945), for example, Horace Cayton and St. Clair Drake described "Race Men" as those men who, with sincerity, sought the advancement of the race. These men invoked racial solidarity and cultivated racial pride, which carried with them ideas of ethical obligation to other African Americans and a duty to "represent" the race in deed and action. Such men, no matter their station, could become heroes, Cayton and Drake maintained, if they dared to challenge and "[beat] the white man at his own game or [force] the white world to recognize his talent or service or achievement."[30] These men could also easily become race hustlers: those who exploited appeals to racial pride for their own selfish gain.[31]

Ellison's "Renaissance Men" are of a different sort. The limit conditions of Black life are readily apparent in his account, but these conditions do not define Black life in toto. Instead, the frontier of Oklahoma, Ellison would have us believe, afforded him and his childhood friends an opportunity to create themselves anew, to reach beyond the narrow confines of Jim Crow, and to imagine a more expansive self: "We were seeking examples, patterns to live by, out of a freedom, which for all its being ignored by the sociologists and subtle thinkers was implicit in the Negro situation. . . . We fabricated our own heroes and ideals catch-as-catch can, and with an outrageous and irreverent sense of freedom."[32] The "Renaissance Man" evoked a sense of being at home in a world that devalued and generally disregarded Black people. It was a heroic assertion of individuality and self-possession among a cadre of "fatherless" boys who decided, despite their circumstances, "to be whoever we would and could be and do anything and everything which other boys did, and do it better."[33] The "Renaissance Man" reconstructs Emerson's notion of representativeness by exposing the illusion of an "uncontaminated innocence" (a young Emerson's words, not my own) that, in its ideological workings, attempts to cut short the life possibilities of America's darker souls.[34] That innocence (Ellison called it hubris) ignored, and ignores, the reality of white supremacy and its constraining effects on the task of self-creation. Emerson powerfully insisted on the limited use of heroes because "the law of individuality collects its secret strength: you are you, and I am I, and so we remain."[35] But that individuality, especially in the United States, is always located in a present soaked in racial history and shaped by choices that color our efforts to live distinctive lives. Du Bois's "two unreconciled strivings" returns as the strenuous task of self-creation behind the veil or across the railroad tracks. The idea of the "Renaissance Man" then stands as a powerful counterweight to Emerson's blind spots: a symbol of possibility—heroic possibility—rooted in the very dynamic of African American culture, which for Ellison, *is* American culture.

The difference between "Race Men" and "Renaissance Men" can be readily seen: the disposition of the former directs us to the political realities of a racist state; the latter to the daunting task of the art of living under captive conditions.

For Ellison, and for someone like Albert Murray, the challenge entails resisting the temptation to reduce African American life to the evil of white supremacy or to define our doings and sufferings solely in terms of what Ellison called sociology or to what Murray referred to as social science fiction, the Marxist/Freudian variant of American protest literature.[36] Both insisted, and rightly so, that we are more complex than that, and both rejected giving the realities of American racism center stage in our effort at self-making. One need not embrace completely their politics to see the power of this claim. We are not sacks and stomachs when it comes to the evils of the white world. I am I; you are you.

———————

With Ellison and Murray in mind, what if the problem is no longer that of protest literature or a politics that reduces individuals to angry, flat characters who murder white women and later grow Afros and give fiery speeches? What if the very condition for the possibility of heroic action has slipped from view, and we are left with a flaccid Black liberalism standing in for *all* Black politics? What if a form of Black moralism blocks the way to how we, how I, might answer the questions "Who am I, what am I, how did I come to be? What shall I make of the life around me . . . ? What does American society *mean* when regarded out of my own eyes, when informed by my *own* sense of the past and viewed by my *own* complex sense of the present?"[37] Answers to these questions make possible representative figures who take up an original relation to the universe.

Remember that moment in Emerson's *Nature*? "Our age is retrospective. It builds sepulchres of the fathers. It writes biographies, histories, and criticism. The foregoing generations beheld God and nature face to face; we, through their eyes." But then Emerson asks irreverent and impious questions: "Why should not we also enjoy an original relation to the universe? Why should not we have a poetry and philosophy of insight and not of tradition and religion by revelation to us, and the history of theirs? . . . The sun shines today also. There is more wool and flax in the fields. There are new lands, new men, new thoughts. Let us demand our own works, and laws and worship." If this is to be so, for me at least, the difficult task, it would seem, involves turning to my first real hero, Malcolm X, the figure who stood in for a father beyond my reach and who set the terms for my political self-understanding. Grappling with his life, citing him (in Walter Benjamin's sense of citation) in my own manic effort to forge a self under present conditions, may just be the path to momentary salvation.

The Humanization of the Sublime: Malcolm X

Malcolm's life is the stuff of lore. His autobiography stands as a canonical text in American letters, introducing young and older readers to an extraordinary journey of self-creation. The backdrop to this story, of course, is Malcolm's role in the Nation of Islam (NOI), an organization quite skeptical, to put the point mildly, of the United States, as well as his strident criticisms of white supremacy during the brief period after his departure from the NOI. We encounter in the narrative a figure of heroic stature, a paragon of Black masculinity daring to speak truthfully to white *and* Black folks. In the words of Ossie Davis's powerful eulogy: "Malcolm was our manhood, our living black manhood! This was his meaning to his people. And, in honoring him, we honor the best in ourselves."

This view captures beautifully my own embrace of the *Autobiography*. There I found a language to interpret my father's rage. He could not stand white people either, and perhaps that anger was at the root of his distance from us, from me. Unlike Malcolm, my father did not channel his rage into acting on behalf of the liberation of Black people. Instead, he delivered mail, took care of his family, and deposited a generalized fear in me that I have had to work hard to hide. Malcolm became then a surrogate father; his words offered a vivid picture of the kind of self I needed to create in order to become a man who would not be defined by a broken relationship with his father.

I had my first conversion experience during the summer of 1986 at Morehouse College, the alma mater of Dr. Martin Luther King Jr. I had just finished reading Malcolm X's autobiography and become convinced that a certain form of Black nationalism was Black America's saving grace. The book affirmed a growing suspicion I had about American democracy. I began to understand

America as a nation consumed by white supremacy. I also felt that if Black people were to achieve a modicum of sanity and well-being, they had to reject this country: that our allegiance had to be to ourselves because the necessary condition for the flourishing of American democracy was the subordination of Black people. One might describe this as a kind of proto-Afro-pessimist view. I made a choice. In theory, America was simply not for me, and a particular form of Black nationalist politics became the way I articulated this rejection. This was indeed a conversion; it was a radical transformation of the heart that expressed itself in the way I lived my life.

I stopped doing what ordinary college students do. I read Harold Cruse, Chiekh Anta Diop, George James, Walter Rodney, and other figures in the Black nationalist canon. I reorganized my relationships and socialized only with like-minded persons. I noticed they all comported themselves in a certain way. So I did too. They even had a peculiar scent. I rubbed my neck with these incense sticks that smelled like nationalists because I did not know oils were the source of the revolutionary's odor. I was, after all, from a small town on the coast of Mississippi where the paper mill and the porgy fish plant provided smells most familiar to me. Black nationalist pieties were about as foreign as Islam.

But my conversion to Black nationalism marked a beginning: a way of defining myself as a "man" over and against the overbearing presence of my father's image. What better path to take than a politics that assumed manliness as a prerequisite for entrée into "the community of saints"—a performance of unfettered masculinity where Black boys could be "men" as they challenged white boys in the "manly" game of politics? My own understanding of Black radicalism then was bound up in the languages and images of the Black nationalism(s) of the 1960s and 1970s. My romance deep-

ened. In order to be militant, to not be my father, I *had* to be Malcolm. I bought horn-rim glasses. I grew my goatee (I still have it),
and I lost myself in the imitation of my hero.

The success of the *Autobiography* stems, in part, from its di-
gestibility. The narrative reads somewhat like the rags-to-riches
stories of the late nineteenth century. From orphan to international leader, from small-time hustler to one of the most important political voices of the twentieth century, Malcolm's life story
is, much like the NOI itself, a quintessentially American story,
where the most powerful people and events happen in the most
unexpected places. In his Pulitzer Prize–winning biography,
Malcolm X: A Life of Reinvention, Manning Marable makes
much of the constructed nature of the *Autobiography* and Alex
Haley's role in making Malcolm X acceptable to mainstream
American society. More specifically, Marable discusses the missing
final chapters of the book and Haley's complicity in what can
only be seen as a government-derived effort to cast Malcolm X in
a particular light. Marable writes: "The basic approach agreed
upon by the FBI and Alfred Balk [a white journalist who co-
authored an article on the NOI with Haley] in late 1962—to give
a reasonably accurate depiction of the Nation of Islam but to
represent the black separatist group as a product of American
society's failure to implement liberal integration—remained
Haley's consistent, overriding ideological objective in the *Autobiography*. Much important information that seemed to diverge
from this central thesis was deleted from the narrative."[38] For
Marable, reclaiming Malcolm X from the distortion of the *Autobiography* constituted an important act of pietistic recovery: a
historical reclamation of a heroic figure from the domesticating
effects of the very vehicle that launched him into a broader political
imaginary.

The irony here is glaring. Marable's biography, published just a few days after his death, has been derided by many as impious. Some questioned his inclusion of the suggestion that Malcolm engaged in homosexual behavior, and others disliked his account of Malcolm's marriage to Betty Shabazz. Such details, they seem to suggest, dulled the image of "our shining black prince" and when joined with the other details of the book made Malcolm X all too human. But my interests in the *Autobiography*, unlike Marable's, are not rooted in a search for an authentic or truer account of Malcolm X. Instead, I am intrigued by how the *Autobiography* works in shaping our reception of him as a heroic figure (how the book cast its spell on me), mindful all the while of what Angela Davis rightly describes as the one-dimensional iconization of Malcolm as a commodity for consumption.[39]

The *Autobiography* works in at least two ways in establishing Malcolm's moral standing. On the one hand, it serves as an example of spiritual autobiography. Malcolm charts his journey from debased criminal on the margins of any moral order to a devout Muslim. I am thinking here of St. Augustine's *Confessions*, written in AD 397. In the first ten books of this work Augustine relates the story of his childhood in Numidia; his licentious youth and early manhood in Carthage, Rome, and Milan, and his bouts with the prevalence of evil within himself and in the world.[40] It is a story of sinner turned priest. Malcolm's autobiography works similarly. We are confronted with two profound conversion experiences. The first led him from small-time criminal to Elijah Muhammed and the NOI; and the second, as it is represented by Haley, from the Black supremacist position of the NOI to a more "universal" embrace of Sunni Islam. The second conversion enables Malcolm X as an exemplary figure to step out of the narrowness of the NOI, which for most white Americans was and remains unintelligible. (Remember James Baldwin felt the need to translate the NOI into the familiar. He wrote in *The Fire Next Time:* "Its emotional tone is as familiar to me as my own skin: it is but another way of saying that sinners shall be bound in hell a thousand years. That sinners have always, for American Negroes, been white is a truth we needn't labor.")[41]

But the book is not simply a spiritual autobiography. The history and continued presence of racism in American life connects it, as Arnold Rampersad notes, to slave narratives and the style of writing indebted to the form that is so familiar to many of us.[42] Emphasizing this dimension of the book turns our attention away from Malcolm as a religious exemplar; instead, we are confronted with a more secular, heroic figure. Here I am reminded of Rousseau's *Confessions,* a story about his journey from international fame to wandering exile, persecution, and alienation, which models a certain view of the virtuous, modern man.[43] With Rousseau we see defiance and vulnerability, passion and confusion, critical examination and denial—the stuff of good autobiography. But Rousseau's *Confessions* is thoroughly secular, and to read the *Autobiography* in this way registers the work of the text outside of a religious framework.

Malcolm is cast simultaneously as a religious exemplar and as a secular prophet. Both solidify his standing as a heroic figure. What is striking about the *Autobiography* read in both registers—the spiritual *and* secular—is that the dynamism of Malcolm X's life gets lodged in the moral lesson contained therein and, as such, he becomes the possession of a wide range of publics with very different commitments (e.g., Muslims, socialists, pan-Africanists, cultural nationalists). In other words, the *Autobiography,* at least today, works to confirm Malcolm's heroic status: it fixes him in his virtue and predetermines, as best as it can, how that virtue speaks to us as readers.

We come to know Malcolm X as hero through a broader narrative about African American struggle. He stands alongside others like Dr. Martin Luther King Jr. whose sacrifices make us possible. And it is in the relationship to that past—its purchase on our moral and ethical sensibilities—that Black people, or at least some Black people, come to understand themselves as particular kinds of agents. How we remember is fraught with ethical significance precisely because those memories orient us to the present and often set our course for future action. Collective memories of a heroic struggle, as Michael Eric Dyson puts the point, can stimulate and preserve cultural achievement. Dyson goes on to argue that "from slavery until the present, African American heroes have been instrumental in preserving the collective memory of black culture against the detrimental consequences of racial amnesia while fighting racism in American public culture."[44] These memories are not simply backward-looking. They orient us to the future as well.

Acknowledgment of past sacrifices constitutes an act of piety—that is, the recognition of heroic lives as sources for whom we take ourselves to be. That recognition, like any gesture to the past, can consume us. We can become lost in the immensity of the personality and our own individual qualities are diminished. Exemplars are curious in this way. They both inspire and potentially enslave. We must work then to strike the right balance between admiration and self-trust, not succumbing to the temptation of idolatry that blinds us to our own unique excellences and potential greatness. Instead, our orientation to the past and its exemplars, like Malcolm, must consist in a lively relation, one in which our thinking remains open-ended and where the imaginative recovery of the past—its citation, as I mentioned in Chapter 1—potentially disrupts current justifications of the order of things.

This is the astonishing achievement of Marable's biography. What is valued here is not a kind of certainty about political matters or the power of rhetorical excess evident in Malcolm X's invective. Instead, Malcolm's life is transformed from that of hero to that of a representative figure engaged in the unnerving task of self-creation. Throughout the biography, as Imani Perry once told me, we find Malcolm "flailing and failing" over and over again; he is alone and betrayed, and yet he constantly reaches for a higher self. With this, the *Autobiography* is not displaced by a *truer* account of Malcolm's life; rather, it is confronted by the frail humanity of its subject. The former demands imitation, the latter solidarity. The moralism of the former casts us as epigones; the latter as co-creators, potentially at least, of a better world.

When understood in this way, Malcolm now stands as wounded as I am. He is recognizable not as a surrogate father but as an exemplar of an examined life lived. The wounds no longer need to be hidden. They must be *tended to* with care. This orientation undermines the masculinist politics that undergirds the heroic representation of Malcolm X. Instead of bowing to a "shining black prince," we confront a wounded, vulnerable Black man courageously fighting with others and reaching for higher levels of excellence.[45] Seeing him wounded in public with others dismisses attributions of divine favor and instead locates the representative figure squarely in the mess with the rest of us. It is the kind of disposition requisite for the politics of tending I believe Ella Baker exemplified.

How then ought we to understand Malcolm as a representative figure? We must find in his *wounded witness* those characteristics worthy of our own moment. Not to imitate them, but to enact those traits in our living in pursuit of justice, because, in fact, they are evident in our characters. Malcolm was a tinkerer—an experimentalist at his core—tending to the needs of those whom he powerfully described as "the rejected and the despised." Dyson has it right when he says, "Malcolm's greatest contribution to us is to *think for ourselves,* to learn to help ourselves when others refuse and to demand a world in which such help is not the preserve of the privileged, but the domain of [everyday, ordinary folks]."[46] To think of Malcolm otherwise is to make of him a sedative, and then to take the pill.

The delicate balance between piety, wound, and self-creation is found in the very effort to forge a unique life in the context of a world, at best, indifferent to our aims and ambitions and, at worst, hostile to our existence. Such a life is funded by past experiences that inform our fits and starts and by the prospects of a future that lies just beyond our fingertips. In his 1990 Nobel lecture, Octavio Paz captured what I am reaching for here in his reflections on the relation of tradition to modernity—echoing, in a way, T. S. Eliot's "Tradition and the Individual Talent." For Paz, "Between tradition and modernity there is a bridge. When they are mutually isolated, tradition stagnates and modernity vaporizes; when in conjunction, modernity breathes life into tradition, while the latter replies with depth and gravity." He goes on to say that "reflecting on the now does not imply relinquishing the future or forgetting the past: *the present is the meeting place for the three directions of time.*"[47] It is here, *right here,* where the depth of our past informs heroic efforts by the most unlikely of persons to speak prophetically to the challenges of now. And it is with this insight that I turn to the philosophy of Ella Baker.

3

ON DEMOCRACY AND ELLA BAKER

It is lonesome, yes. For we are the last of the loud.
Nevertheless, live.
Conduct your blooming in the noise and whip of the
    whirlwind.

GWENDOLYN BROOKS, *IN THE MECCA*

Ella Baker, Pragmatism, and
Black Democratic Perfectionism

On April 16, 1960, in Raleigh, North Carolina, at Shaw University, students who had participated in lunch counter sit-ins throughout the South gathered to found what would become the Student Nonviolent Coordinating Committee (SNCC). The founding conference had been organized by Ella Baker, executive director of the Southern Christian Leadership Conference. Baker, a seasoned organizer, sought to bring Black student activists together to enable them "TO SHARE experience gained in recent protest demonstrations and TO HELP chart future goals for effective action."[1] She would hold off attempts by Dr. Martin Luther King Jr. and others to absorb the energy of the students into established civil rights organizations, and provide space for the voicing of a different kind of Black politics rooted in the democratic energy of young students who dared to challenge Jim Crow directly.

Baker believed, and she enacted this belief in the way she organized, that what the Black freedom struggle needed most, what America needed most, was "the development of people who are interested not in being leaders as much as in developing leadership among other people."[2] She had come to understand that the model of leadership represented by Dr. King and the preachers around him inclined people to a kind of hero-worship, which blinded them to their own capacities and responsibilities. Baker voiced then a deep-seated suspicion of the work of charismatic leadership—not to deny its productive potential (after all she was a charismatic figure of sorts), but to be mindful of how charisma can short-circuit democratic energies.[3] "Instead of the leader as a person who was supposed to be a magic man," she argued, "you could develop individuals bound together by a concept that benefitted the larger numbers and provided an opportunity for them to grow into being responsible for carrying out a program."[4] The challenge was to help others develop their unique selves and to bring to the fore their potential as problem-solving agents. As Baker noted, "My basic sense of it has always been to get people to understand that in the long run they themselves are the only protection they have against violence or injustice. . . . *People have to be made to understand that they cannot look for salvation anywhere but to themselves.*"[5] This realization depends upon encounters through critical participation that can generate self-trust, which enables collective efforts among the most unlikely of agents to transform unjust conditions. This view undermines traditional models of prophetic and heroic leadership that condition us to look through the eyes of others. Instead, we come to hold the view, as

Emerson insisted in an exquisite riff on the Parable of the Talents, "that though the wide universe is full of good, no kernel of nourishing corn can come to him but through his toil bestowed on that plot of ground which is given to him to till."[6]

Baker commends a view of leadership commensurate with my efforts to reconstruct our understanding of the prophetic and the heroic. She put the point quite powerfully:

> In . . . political life I have always felt it was a handicap for oppressed peoples to depend so largely upon a leader, because unfortunately in our culture, the charismatic leader usually becomes a leader because he has found a spot in the public limelight. It usually means he has been touted through the public media, which means that the media made him, and the media may undo him. There is also the danger in our culture that, because a person is called upon to give public statements and is acclaimed by the establishment, such a person gets to the point of believing that he is the movement. Such people get so involved with playing the game of being important that they exhaust themselves and their time, and they don't do the work of actually organizing people.[7]

Our attention must turn from the glare of the supposed gifts of the prophet and hero toward the cultivation of dispositions requisite for genuine democratic life. For Baker, each of us has a moral imagination; each of us can in fact, no matter our material circumstances, engage in reflective efforts to reach beyond the challenges / constraints of the current moment and grasp undisclosed opportunities that can, without guarantee, upend the order of things and make possible new ideals and ends. We do not need "*the* prophet" or "*the* hero" for this. What we need, above all, and this is not always self-evident, is trust in ourselves—at least this is how I understand Baker's famous dictum: "Strong people don't need strong leaders."[8] The cultivation of self-trust—resulting in a robust sense of individuality *within* community—becomes the basis for democratic collective action and allows for a multitude of prophetic and heroic moments.

I want to offer a reading of Baker that extends the reach of my peculiar embrace of pragmatism. As I mentioned in Chapter 1, my view is indebted to Cornel West's understanding of prophetic pragmatism. West has it right when he says that a consequence of the Emersonian evasion of philosophy is a culture of creative democracy "where politically adjudicated forms of knowledge are produced in which human participation is encouraged and for which human personalities are enhanced."[9] What was once the purview of philosophers now becomes the work of each of us, and, for West, "the populace deliberating is creative democracy in the making." This does not mean that professional elites are always the object of scorn or that mob rule is the order of the day. "Rather," he argues, "it is the citizenry in action, with its civil consciousness molded by participation in public-interest-centered and individual-right-regarding democracy." Prophetic pragmatism thematizes the political implications of the "Emersonian swerve." It yokes pragmatism more closely to the philosophy of John Dewey by insisting that it be understood as a form of cultural criticism and that its idea of politics make central the experiences of everyday, ordinary people.[10]

I have resonated with this view ever since I first heard it as a graduate student, but I remain suspicious of West's use of the word "prophetic" and the view of leadership it often presupposes (perhaps, the problem rests with the ghost of Kierkegaard that seemingly haunts West's embrace of pragmatism and leads him to ask certain questions that I believe are best left aside). I have sought to read the prophetic in a register shorn of its romance with genius and released from its indebtedness to a certain view of the Hebrew prophets. I locate the prophetic function in the very exercise of critical intelligence—to see it as the work of the moral imagination envisioning beyond the immediate circumstances of our living (a dramatic rehearsal in the service of justice). In Chapter 2, a leveling impulse motivated my efforts to think of the heroic in terms of representativeness rooted in vulnerability and wound, a view that brings us all into its orbit as the occasion may arise for each of us to exhibit such a quality.

My intent has been, and it remains, to insist on those conditions that enable us to step out from under the shadows of past giants in order to address imaginatively the challenges of our day in voices uniquely our own. My concern about West's use of the prophetic, beyond its supplemental function, is that it threatens to undo the insight: that the prophet's voice all too often drowns out the deliberating populace and simply calls us to drop our spades and to follow him.[11] Much more is required in the pursuit of worthwhile ends and in the cultivation of capacities for the exercise of deliberative and practical reasoning.

I want to read Baker as an exemplar of prophetic pragmatism shorn of the anxieties that haunt its initial articulation. Her life's witness helps me reconstruct what we might mean when we invoke the phrase and, more importantly, it makes explicit a view of Black democratic perfectionism I want to commend—that is, an embrace of self-cultivation in the pursuit of justice. Of course, as Barbara Ransby notes, "Baker never wrote an organizing manual or an ideological treatise[;] her theory was literally inscribed in her daily work—her practice."[12] This is precisely the strength of Baker's view; it is tested in the context of lived experience and in the light of actual problems faced. Hers is a view that cannot be accused of failing to take seriously the operations of power, precisely because it was developed (and enacted) in the throes of power's exercise. In this sense, Baker's pragmatic witness escapes some of the concerns about pragmatism more generally: that it is naïve about self-interest and corporate power, or, more generally, blind to the agonistic dimensions of democratic life.

Ransby reaches for theoretical frames elsewhere to account for Baker's philosophy: Antonio Gramsci, C. L. R. James, and Paulo Freire help her make sense of the radically democratic thrust of Baker's practice. I prefer to place her in conversation with Sheldon Wolin and his politics of tending, not only to amplify her views but to correct the blind spots in Wolin's account. I also want to suggest that Baker's insistence on the capacities and responsibilities of everyday, ordinary people and her tireless work on behalf of what I take to be creative democracy is best understood in pragmatist terms. Three slogans guide my efforts to read Baker in this way: *a chastened voluntarism; a morally motivated experimentalism;* and *a view of democracy as an ethical way of life.*

At the heart of Baker's philosophy rests a chastened voluntarist impulse that informs a militant egalitarianism. I say "chastened" because Baker, like James Baldwin, fully understood that human capacities take shape in contexts and situations that often dash dreams and deny individuals dignity and standing—contexts that socialize individuals into doubting themselves and their abilities. Baldwin's words in "The Uses of the Blues" (1964) come to mind:

> I'm talking about what happens to you if, having barely escaped suicide, or death, or madness, or yourself, you watch your children growing up and no matter what you do, no matter what you do, you are powerless . . . against the force

of the world that is out to tell your child that he has no right to be alive. . . . In every generation, ever since Negroes have been here, every Negro mother and father has had to face that child and try to create in that child some way of surviving this particular world, some way to make the child who will be despised not despise himself.[13]

Baker's is not a view of Promethean powers deployed in a naïvely romantic act of self-creation. For her, the reach for a higher self entails a struggle, not simply with the dangers of conformity but with the conditions that block the way to our understanding of who we can be and what we are capable of. The conditions that keep us from flying. The primacy of human will and practice remains but is shadowed by the persistence of evils that frustrate our self-realization. The task is to develop one's unique talents within community and to understand those talents as gifts capable of transforming the circumstances of one's living with others in the face of such evils. Baker insists on the value of each human being and their ability, if acknowledged and cultivated, to contribute to making a better world. This is not a position of an undifferentiated mass;[14] her view is a naturalized understanding of the dignity and worth of each individual and the sanctity of their capacity to do good in a world shot through with ugliness.

Baker's militant egalitarianism stands alongside her morally motivated experimentalism. Her practice involved efforts to select future experience with the understanding of the possibility of error when we act. Nothing was settled beforehand and what was required was a willingness to experiment—to tinker—with an inheritance while understanding that the future is implicated in the present. In this light, ideals were pursued in the context of receptive practice *close to the ground*. She encouraged listening, adjusting, and adapting in the pursuit of collectively shared ends. Drawing on the insight of Charles Paynes's *I've Got the Light of Freedom*, Romand Coles notes that "Baker sought to cultivate a profound 'openness to experience' on the part of the organizers she helped teach: a strong sense that this was a chief quality that they themselves should seek to practice and engender in their efforts to organize radical-democratic communities of struggle."[15] Openness to experience placed in the foreground the necessity of process or method. For Baker, the ends for which they struggled required a similar commitment to the means by which those ends would be attained. If the means by which we seek a more expansive democratic life are in fact authoritarian, the seeds of the undoing of any good are present from the beginning. Means matter. Otherwise those who fight for good today turn out to be the tyrants of tomorrow. Processes that are liberating today end up tightening the vice grip of our domination. Baker insisted that democratic and participatory values be the basis of Black political struggle for this reason.[16] As Dewey stated in his 1937 essay "Democracy Is Radical," "The fundamental principle of democracy is that the ends of freedom and individuality for all can be attained only by the means that accord with those ends."[17] Otherwise we end up with tyrants dismissive of democratic virtue or browbeating moralists who treat most like the herd.

Baker rejected top-down models of leadership and encouraged a patient, inclusive deliberative process that embodied the militant egalitarianism noted above. Each voice was valued. Every thought warranted recognition and attention. As SNCC organizer Mary King put it: "We had a stern insistence that our conceptualization, our thinking, our framework, should grow from engagement with the people that we were working with rather than from doctrine or any ready-made philosophy."[18] Or, as Barbara

Jones recalled, "There was no room for talking down to anyone. There was never the expressed attitude that a person who was illiterate had something less to offer."[19] An openness to the possibilities inherent in experience characterized their practice. At the heart of this form of organizing were "quotidian rituals engendering individual and collective cultivation of responsive democratic character."[20]

Finally, Baker understood that democracy is more than a body of procedures and certainly is not reducible to the principles of liberalism. Instead, democracy carries with it the radical notion that every individual, no matter their station in life, is capable of exercising responsibility. Democracy, on this view, is an ethical ideal bound up with a particular idea of self-cultivation and rooted in a faith in the capacities of human beings for intelligent judgment and action. Individuals need only be empowered to look within themselves and to their experiences with others to grasp fully ideas of value that orient them to social and political realities.[21]

The late Bob Moses, the famed SNCC organizer, insisted that the revolutionary work of SNCC resided not simply in its efforts to dismantle Jim Crow, but principally in whom they brought into the political process. He recounted the story of SNCC field secretaries in a federal courtroom in Greenwood, Mississippi, "packed with black sharecroppers . . . hushed along its walls, packed onto its benches, and [attending] to the question put by Federal District Judge Clayton: 'Why is SNCC taking illiterates down to register to vote?'"[22] Those illiterate Black sharecroppers brought to that courthouse and to the ballot box a wealth of experience that shaped their demands of the state, informed their embrace of democratic ideals, and expanded, if only for a moment, our understanding of who we take ourselves to be as a nation. Moses, like Baker, understood that genuine, creative democracy called not only for the pursuit of worthwhile ends but for the pursuit of the ends in ways that enlisted those often pushed to the margins and who lived in the cracks and crevices of our society. The language echoes Dewey's, but the words are given depth and power, I believe, in a practice shaped by Baker's view.

Dewey held that democracy understood as an ethical ideal entails the deliberate work of forging bonds of association in such a way that the capacities and powers of every individual are realizable in full participation in political and cultural life. Democracy extends beyond the mere exercise of public reason. It is not just the act of deliberating with our fellows about important matters or participation in elections informed by a flood of talk. Democracy requires a richly textured democratic culture close to the ground, where the habits and dispositions necessary for its flourishing are alive in the experiences of everyday, ordinary folk. Much of American life, especially under neoliberal conditions,[23] frustrates these ends: from the destabilizing currents of rapid modernization that "dislocate and unsettle local communities" to the attitudes and practices rooted in white supremacy and patriarchy that often "made shambles of American democracy." What is needed—required even—under such conditions are innovative and creative ways of revitalizing local communities and fostering "the development of multiple publics where citizens [can] engage in debate and deliberation together."[24]

Baker's radical democratic philosophy entailed what I want to call her "networked democratic localism." The phrase is a bit awkward, but I think it captures the approach to democratic politics based in encounters in multiple, local publics. Such encounters expanded possibility through critical participation in challenging Jim Crow and in the cultivation of democratic dispositions and habits among those who struggled together. But this view should not be read as conceding the national political terrain to others: the invocation of localism was not to deny the relevance of the national scene (although it certainly indicated suspicion).[25] Instead, actions in one local setting link up practices elsewhere that, together, had national implications. Just as Ella Baker's organizing for the National Association for the Advancement of Colored People took her all over the South, establishing pathways, connections, and conduits that connected her practice across geographies, a more generalized understanding of democratic localism presumed the circulation of practices and ideas along a network of efforts to address particular problems in light of specific situations.[26] Collectively, such efforts constituted loosely a national thrust. Separately, the substance of the practice was evidenced in the receptive orientation close to the ground, in what I called in Chapter 1 the "readying of the self" to engage courageously and intelligently for transformative action (revealing an idea of democracy as an ethical way of life).

I agree with Barbara Ransby when she says that Baker's "political praxis reflected a deliberative model. Interaction, discussion, debate, and consensus building were key components of that praxis. In contrast, voting, lobbying the corridors of power, and getting favored candidates elected were secondary considerations."[27] But Ransby doesn't identify the Black democratic perfectionist strand of Baker's localism: that her practice entailed a radical commitment to the cultivation of democratic individuality among Black people in the service of justice. Baker's politics cannot be contained by a deliberative model alone. Much more is going on: the aim is for the emergence of an indigenous cadre of leaders capable of finding salvation in and for themselves and who, by extension, would constitute a wholesale assault on a particular model of Black leadership that resists accountability by those perceived as an undifferentiated mass.

Baker's practice involved aspirational claims (i.e., claims about what kind of society we hoped to live in and what kind of persons we aspired to be) as well as historical claims, rooted in care, about the context of where we now stand (i.e., claims about the enduring legacy of white supremacy that deforms self-formation and about the history of struggle against white supremacy that constitutes the backdrop of current efforts). Her democratic perfectionism is situated in the histories of Black life, stories that narrate the litany of events, and the chorus of Black voices struggling for freedom and resisting domination. These histories carry with them an *ethical ought:* that the struggle and sacrifices of so many require of those who are its immediate beneficiaries a commitment to treating one's fellows justly and to ensuring a society where all can flourish. To act otherwise is to risk the troublesome label of race traitor.

Invocations of that history can spur or constrain. They can serve as wind beneath our wings in the context of imaginative engagement with the present or they can limit the range of actions to an ossified set of practices that no longer best represent our efforts. Baker's Black democratic perfectionism commended the former. Just as she resisted efforts to absorb the student movement into older, established civil rights organizations, Baker insisted on the space for the young people of SNCC to find their own voices and to make their unique contributions to a tradition of struggle. Here the citation of the past, not a nostalgic longing for origins, gave shape and contour to their imaginings. It did not readily deform and distort.

Baker's attentiveness to the cultivation of democratic dispositions among the least of these is best described, following the
political philosopher Sheldon Wolin, as *a politics of tending*. As
Wolin writes, "The idea of tending is one that centers politics
around practices, that is, around the habits of competence or skill
that are routinely required if things are to be taken care of." He
goes on to say "that tending is tempered by the feeling of concern
for objects whose nature requires that they be treated as historical
and biographical beings. The beings are such as to need regular
attention from someone who is concerned about well-being and is
sensitive to historical needs."[28] Imagination as an act of empathy is
central to the politics of tending in that it opens us up to the wounds
and joys of strangers, enables habit formation that affirms the dignity
of our fellows, and encourages a willingness to embrace receptive
practices of listening and of "being still" as critical features of a
mode of democratic struggle.

Tending gathers politics around rooted, knotted practices—
doings and sufferings that evidence habits and dispositions forged
over a life lived. To be open to such experience is to tend to roughly
hewn hands that mark a life of toil, to bloodshot eyes that signal
too much drink, to raucous laughter that offers a glimpse of the
depths of joy, and to tend to the blank stare that reveals either
defeat or possibility. Tending can be expressed in Ella Baker's
powerful question she often asked when meeting someone, even
when her memories had long faded: "Who are your people?" The
question subverts a sociology, as Ralph Ellison would put it, that
reduces the depth of Black experiences to flat statistics of pathology by, instead, seeking an account of love and wound that
constitute the ground beneath one's feet and set in place the
conditions of possibility for a higher self.[29]

I do not want to assimilate Baker's view wholly into Wolin's. In fact, reading Wolin alongside Baker offers a profound corrective to his view of fugitive democracy and deepens our understanding of the politics of tending.

Sheldon Wolin and Fugitive Democracy

Much has been said about Sheldon Wolin's provocative view of fugitive democracy. Wolin views democracy "as a mode of being which is conditioned by bitter experience, doomed to succeed only temporarily, but is a recurrent possibility as long as memory of the political survives."[30] "Memory" here refers to the invocation of efforts by everyday, ordinary citizens joined together in pursuit of commonly shared ends "to promote or protect the well-being of the collectivity."[31]

Such moments have become increasingly rare, making our recollection and invocation of them even more important. Wolin tells a dark story of loss as corporativist superpower saturates / distorts our ways of living, where deep and persistent inequalities of power, status, and income cast our fellows into the shadows and keep them there as ideas of disposable people become as commonplace as the Walmarts that may hire them or the prisons that may house them. Here government divests itself of its welfare function and expands its policing function. Political economy dominates. His is a story where "citizens" give way to "nervous subjects" or "imperial citizens" who are depoliticized and passive, where an "inverted regime promotes a sense of weakness, a collective futility that culminates in the erosion of the democratic faith, in political apathy, and the privatization of the self," and, I might add, in the privatization of social misery.[32]

Against the backdrop of this bleak picture, democracy as Wolin portrays it is episodic and rare. It is "a moment of experience, a crystallized response to deeply felt grievances or needs on the part of those whose main preoccupation—demanding time and energy—is to scratch out a decent existence. Its moment is not just a measure of fleeting time but an action that protests actualities and reveals possibilities."[33] One might think of Wolin's view of democracy as a kind of *political hierophany,* an eruption of democratic energies that "activate[s] the demos and destroy[s] the boundaries that bar access to political experience."[34] Democracy unsettles, destabilizes, and redraws boundaries—revealing "that ordinary individuals are capable of creating new cultural patterns of commonality at any moment."[35]

These everyday people are not the unencumbered selves so central to the fantasies of liberalism but persons formed and shaped within particular places and by the myriad things they do and the choices they make in the social worlds they inhabit.[36] Who these ordinary people take themselves to be is deeply bound up with the complicated and often menacing histories that shape how they see the world and understand themselves. Their identities are always located in some place and time. They are not "abstract disconnected bearers of rights, privileges and immunities" but rather living, breathing persons with joys and wounded attachments, persons who "draw sustenance from circumscribed relationships: family, friends, church, neighborhood, workplace, community, town, city."[37] When these individuals act together to imagine and enact new possibilities, they experience "a democratic moment and contribute to the discovery, care, and *tending* of a commonality of shared concerns." And in these moments "the political lives," although commonality remains "fugitive and impermanent."[38]

For Wolin, constitutionalism and representational forms attenuate and arrest democracy.[39] Institutionalization "tends to produce internal hierarchies, to restrict experience, to associate political experience with institutional experience." Both contain and constrain democratic energy. Wolin writes: "Instead of a conception of democracy as indistinguishable from its constitution, I propose accepting the familiar charges that democracy is inherently unstable, inclined toward anarchy, and identified with revolution and using these traits as the basis for a different, *a* constitutional conception of democracy."[40] The object of the political hierophany that is democracy ought not be to seize the state apparatus[41] but rather to contribute to a revitalized localism where the details of our daily lives with others and the memory of those efforts from a distant past call us to join with our fellows in efforts to secure goods for ourselves, for those we hold dear, and for generations to come. Together, we not only have the capacity to imagine a better world right where we currently stand, we can act collectively to make that better world a reality, however fleeting.

Now I don't want to pretend to have captured the full complexity of Wolin's position. His view is far more complicated than what I have presented here (and I have made no attempt to engage his expansive and imaginative readings of an array of philosophers and political theorists, both ancient and modern). But I should note that there have been interesting criticisms of fugitive democracy. Some have expressed concerns over the ambiguity of the concept of the political and his invocation of democracy and its identity with revolution. Others have worried about the scale of the project: that the localism Wolin commends is not sufficient for the size and complexity of modern societies.[42]

For some, the scale of modern societies warrants the intervention of the state, not simply for imposing order and producing internal hierarchies but to improve the lives of those who might otherwise be vulnerable, because they live in close proximity to others who conspire to do them harm. W. E. B. Du Bois's description of the contradiction exemplified by the controversy around the Freedmen's Bureau helps underscore this tension:

> The champions of the bill argued that the strengthening of the Freedmen's Bureau was still a military necessity; that it was needed for the proper carrying out of the Thirteenth Amendment. . . . The opponents of the measure declared that the war was over, and the necessity for war measures past; that the Bureau, by reason of its extraordinary powers, was clearly unconstitutional in time of peace, and was destined to irritate the South and pauperize the freedman, at a final cost of possibly hundreds of millions. These two arguments were unanswered, and indeed unanswerable: *the one that the extraordinary powers of the Bureau threatened the civil rights of all citizens; and the other that the government must have power to do what manifestly must be done, and that present abandonment of the freedmen meant their practical re-enslavement.*[43]

Wolin's vision would not resolve this problem; in fact, at least according to some, his idea of democracy would exacerbate it.

Finally, some critics worry that Wolin's view of democracy as fugitive, as fleeting and episodic, resigns us to a world in which domination is inevitable and inescapable. Here democratic energies predictably subside, and we are left with the nastiness of life as it is, only nominally changed. One wonders how this bleak view, what my colleague Jeffrey Stout describes as "the spirit of spiritless creatures," inspires ordinary people to resist.[44] For these critics, Wolin's darkness consumes his radical democratic vision.[45]

Wolin has the resources to respond to his critics, but I am not interested in vindicating his account here. Instead, I want to push toward a different kind of criticism, one that evades what Stout sees as "his distaste for assuming the responsibilities of governance" or his somber, despairing view of democracy's chances, and instead direct attention to what I take to be a nagging absence in his account: *the absence of a sustained treatment of white supremacy and the actual fugitives it created.*[46]

There is something terribly familiar about Wolin's account of fugitive democracy. Not so much in his appeal to fifth-century Athens; I have always been struck by the need, at least on the part of some white American thinkers, to reach for a distant past for examples of the world they commend to us. The theologian Stanley Hauerwas directed our attention to the early Christians.[47] Wolin to Athens. Both run past the Black folk right in front of their faces. After all, invisibility has been a hallmark of our presence in politics *and* in letters. But when Wolin describes fugitive democracy as "a mode of being which is conditioned by bitter experience," as something "doomed to succeed only temporarily, but is a recurrent possibility," as "a moment of experience, a crystallized response to deeply felt grievances or needs on the part of those whose main preoccupation is to scratch out a decent existence"; when he sees democratic action beginning with "the demos constructing / collecting itself from scattered experiences and fusing these into a self-consciousness about common powerlessness and its causes" and the demos as being "created from a shared realization that powerlessness comes from being shut out of the councils where power's authority is located";[48] when he says, without flinching, that democracy escapes form and ought to be understood instead as "standing opposition"[49]—in these moments of apparent despair and ever-encroaching darkness, Wolin sounds a lot like those Black folk on the underside of the American political project who dared to imagine a democratic future for themselves, for those they hold dear, and for future generations.

Throughout his body of work Wolin acknowledges the realities of American racism and the influence of the civil rights movement on his political theory. But neither takes center stage in his theorizing of the political. The civil rights movement serves as an example of collective action that gathers its power from outside the system, but it does not, for Wolin, rise to the level of sustained theoretical reflection. All too often when Wolin engages the issue directly he slips into a kind of sentimentality about the evil of the institution of slavery or the moral failings of those who embraced it only to point beyond the deadly fact of its presence in American life.[50]

In *Theorizing Race in the Americas,* political theorist Juliet Hooker argues, among other things, that rethinking fugitive democracy in light of the experiences of fugitive slaves and ex-slaves (and I would add those who bore the burden of that inheritance in the actual lives they sought to live well after slavery's demise) "extends and sharpens the concept." She turns to Frederick Douglass, particularly his famous address, "What to the Slave Is the Fourth of July?" (1852), and his autobiographies to complicate the idea of who the democratic citizen is and who she can be. These persons stood betwixt and between; they lived, in effect, *in the breach.* And, for Hooker, that political experience enabled the development of what she calls "enhanced democratic subjectivities because their experience of the democratic more closely maps onto its episodic and insurgent character."[51] Black fugitives in the breach held an outsider status, "as they repudiated both the law and the state that enacted it."

Here she identifies two constitutive features of Black fugitivity that complicate and deepen Wolin's view: (1) that literal (rather than metaphorical) fugitivity of the escaped slave involves a different and fraught relationship with the rule of law and (2) that the myriad ways in which this condition is experienced "might permanently shape political subjectivity." In both instances, the idea of fugitive democracy is read or understood at a different register. Think, for example, of the following moment in Wolin's *Tocqueville between Two Worlds* in which he discusses Tocqueville's use of *moeurs,* those habits and customs so central to the daily political and social life of the country. For Tocqueville, Wolin writes,

> the transmutation of laws and legal practices into *moeurs* was the key to the American political culture. Tocqueville's favorite example of the power of *moeurs* was the circulation throughout society of the legal culture represented by lawyers, judges, and the jury system. "Public men" in America, Tocqueville explained, are typically lawyers and naturally apply "legal habits and turn of mind to public affairs." At the same time, most ordinary Americans have experienced jury service and by means of that "free school" have become accustomed to legal language and adopted it "as a sort of popular language. . . . The juristic spirit, born within schools and courts, is diffused little by little beyond their confines; it infiltrates the whole society, descending into the lowest ranks till finally the whole people have contracted some of the habits and tastes of a magistrate."[52]

But fugitive slaves, and those who dared to resist the systems of racial exclusion that followed, were in fact *lawbreakers.* The condition of slavery produced an incredibly "distorted relationship between the force of law and the political and moral right." Douglass exploited this distortion in his 1852 address, by reading the American Revolution as a violation of the law in the name of higher moral principles, and by describing those who resisted slavery—especially those who, like himself, were literal fugitives from slavery—as exemplars of civic virtue. Hooker writes, "Douglass can be read as suggesting that revolutionary acts of resistance are constitutive to the praxis of democratic citizenship" and reveal "the permanent uneven reach of democracy and the rule of law, as struggles to enlarge the demos are likely to be resisted and viewed as anything but lawful protests."[53]

But it is the second feature of fugitivity that draws my attention. Black fugitivity and its consequences complicate how we might understand the formation of democratic subjectivity. Douglass captures this in his autobiography as he recounts the precariousness of Black freedom:

> Let him be a fugitive in a strange land—a land given up to be the hunting-ground for slaveholders—whose inhabitants are legalized kidnappers—where he is every moment subjected to the terrible liability of being seized upon by his fellow-men . . . I say, let him place himself in my situation . . . among fellow-men, yet feeling in the midst of wild beasts . . . I say let him be placed in this most trying situation—the situation in which I was placed—then, and not till then, will he fully appreciate the hardships of, and know how to sympathize with, the toil-worn and whip-scarred fugitive slave.[54]

Here Douglass anticipates Henry David Thoreau's insistence in *Walden* (1854) on the miracle of "looking through each other's eyes for an instant."[55]

Douglass makes clear that it is within this *haunting* context that the Black fugitive has to freedom dream, a context that is the result—and this cannot be denied without succumbing to an arresting illusion—of the unspeakable doings of white folks, of living "in the midst of wild beasts." The kinds of persons that come into being here, bathed in an intimate experience with precarity because of the nastiness of white folks, as Toni Morrison writes, dramatically affect how democracy is imagined and enacted. That imagining begins with the unsettling assumption that the value gap and the racial habits that give it life have constrained the reach of our concerns, of who is considered worthy, and have stood in the way of our being together since the country's inception.

In my other writings, I have maintained, implicitly at least, that the value gap deforms our characters and blocks the development of the kinds of dispositions that democracy requires.[56] Racial habits[57] are the ways we live the belief[58] that white people are more valued (and are more valuable) than others. They are the things we do, without thinking, that sustain the value gap. Racial habits range from snap judgments we make about Black people that rely on stereotypes to the ways we think about race that we get from living within our respective communities and the various histories that shaped how those communities came into being (recall the Baldwin quotation: "The great force of history comes from the fact that we carry it within us"). We learn racial habits, then, not by way of overt racism, but through the details of daily life in a country whose *moeurs* and built environment have been and continue to be fundamentally shaped by race matters.[59]

Dispositions matter. Character matters. Wolin argues in "The People's Two Bodies" that two different conceptions of "collective identity, of power, and of the terms of power" have animated the American political tradition: one, *the body politic,* emphasizes the active capacities of the people, rooted in democratic energies, as they reject "an established mode of authority" and the other, *a political economy,* is primarily economic and anti-democratic aimed at changing "democratic citizens into beings disposed to render 'obedience to [the federal government's] authority.'"[60] Both emerge out of an attempt to answer the question of who we are as *a people*—about political identity. This is shaped, Wolin maintains, by "the ways a society chooses to generate power and to exercise it." He continues:

> The historical project of most societies, including our own, is to shape its members so that they do more than obey or submit: they become *disposed,* inclined in such a way that political authorities can count on their active support most of the time. These dispositions have to be cultivated if power is to be generated and continuously available. Power depends importantly on an historical accumulation of dispositions. But dispositions are not something so trite as "learned behavior." They are inscribed demands of the kind that the village laborer had to "learn" in the factories and slums. Power is not, therefore, an exchange or a transaction but an *exaction.* It is had on terms that exact over time and become cumulative. . . . The working out of the terms of power *determines* the political identity of the collectivity.[61]

But Wolin fails to note, and I find this baffling given his attentiveness to most matters, that what connects the two bodies—one based in the Declaration of Independence, its charter, and the Articles of

Confederation and the other in the vision of Hamilton and Madison—
is the distorting and deforming effects of the value gap. Dispositions
are being formed and shaped over time, with accumulated advantage,
that produce an idea of "the people" as decidedly and unashamedly
white with all the benefits and burdens that come with being so
and not being so (reminds me of Louis Armstrong's question,
"What did I do to be so black and blue?").

Here one must question Wolin's repeated invocation of community or "the well-being of the collectivity." Nicholas Xenos
worries, and rightly so, that the people's two bodies may smuggle
in a metaphysical notion of "the people" that actually works against
Wolin's insistence on multiple, contested communities. As Xenos
put it, "To conceptualize a mythic communal body is to put forward
an organic image that suggests the realization of its parts in the whole,
an always already existing Community that prefigures and gives
meaning to communities."[62] And, it happens to be the case, especially in the context of thinking theoretically about the modern
world with slavery and colonial expansion as its foundation, that
this "Community" is as white as snow.

The *white,* political identity that emerges from this understanding of "the people" limits the sphere of those people's moral
concern and distorts the very form and content of their democratic imaginings. In the end, Wolin seems to miss how the value
gap limits our capacity for generosity, our sense of humility, our
experience of benevolence and mutuality, and our idea of justice.
The value gap stands in the way of us standing together.[63]

Baker and the Problem of Black Custodial Politics

Closer attention to the democratic energies of Black strivings certainly exposes how "whiteness" gets in the way of the political

under modern conditions. And it is here that I turn back to Baker. To be sure, Wolin posits a politics of tending over and against a politics of intending, and he does so in the context of disrupting how we remember. A politics of tending, to put the point crudely, represents an anti-federalist position while a politics of intending reflects the impulses and efforts of the likes of Madison and Hamilton. Federalists aspire for a form of authority that obscures the richly textured practices of the local; they hide from view an active political life, which preceded the effort to stretch localities into a wider constellation of federal power and the idea of the citizen it required.[64]

Following Tocqueville, Wolin understands these local practices as the lifeblood of American democratic culture. It is here, in the intimate space of the local—what I have been calling close to the ground—that Americans acquire the habits, values, and dispositions requisite for democratic life where "democratic citizenship is a process of becoming," not an already established fact.[65] But for much of African American history, the local has also been the site of terror, for many who embraced the sanctity of the local also defended white supremacy with a vengeance. It is in the very experience of racial terror, in the backbreaking labor discipline of the cotton fields, in the reality of de jure segregation, or in the deadly encounters with police today—the literal, direct experience with power—that "politics as usual" are dispensed with and "the political" is evidenced in a particular kind of democratic possibility.

Baker understood this profoundly (and without taking on the claim about fugitive democracy). She advocated for and enacted the development of democratic practices at the local level informed by the historicity of place and the complexity of the actors involved. What comes into view here is not simply the operations of state power, but the formation of particular kinds of subjects in confrontation with the operations of power. To insist on the capacities and responsibilities of everyday, ordinary people—to urge that they reach for a higher self under conditions of political capture—is to give democratic perfectionism a radical inflection. For Wolin, "democracy requires that the experiences of justice and injustice serve as moments for the demos to think, to reflect, perchance, to construct themselves as actors."[66] For Baker, such moments occasion an opportunity to *expand the very idea of who matters* in the demos and, in the context of political struggle with others, such moments offer an occasion to construct a vision of ourselves as agents and, again, as saviors.

Cornel West agrees with Wolin's general account and readily admits that the commitments of the prophetic pragmatist "to individuality and democracy, historical consciousness and systematic social analyses, and tragic action in an evil-ridden world can take place in—though on the margins of—a variety of traditions."[67] He chooses to find his feet as a prophetic pragmatist (though he has since jettisoned the label) in the Christian tradition. That tradition provides him with existential comfort in the face of the absurd, and it enables an organic connection with the wretched of the earth who, as he puts it, are deeply religious. I have no qualms with West's personal assent to Christian stories. I worry only that the model of leadership he implicitly embraces, one seemingly indebted to the role of the preacher and the way the prophetic sometimes cashes out in the preacher's hands, subverts, under present conditions, the more egalitarian premises he sets forth.

Baker's approach, I believe, evades this problem. Hers is not rooted in the mode of the preacher but in the labor of the many women who worked hard every day to make the mission of the church a reality. To accent her Black democratic perfectionism of-

fers, for me at least, resources for striking the right balance between piety and self-creation and marks a pathway to step out of
the shadows of forms of Black moralism that deny imaginative
and representative action.

The backdrop of my reading of Baker is the ascendance of a
particular form of Black custodial politics exacerbated by neoliberalism, a distinctive form of what Wolin calls a politics of intending. This politics collapses the complexity of Black life into
an undifferentiated mass in need of representation by a Black
political class. It short-circuits the need for substantive deliberation and banishes mechanisms of accountability as Black elites
broker on behalf of Black constituencies whose interests are, so it
would seem to some, readily identifiable. The effect is the demobilization of Black democratic energies, which results in a kind of
nonparticipatory politics as Black people, every election cycle, are
treated as the herd and as some grab megaphones to speak for
them. The politics of tending get tossed in the waste bin.

The story of Black custodial politics is a complex one. Crudely,
it begins with the effects of slavery and Jim Crow in constraining
the very way Black politics is imagined (placing an idea of collective interests and representation of those interests at the heart of
its practice),[68] continues in the transformation of Black politics in
the aftermath of the Black freedom struggles of the 1960s and 1970s,
and culminates in the neoliberal consolidation of a particular
regime of Black representation with the election of Barack Obama.
To include the former president in this story is a provocative claim.
But I want to suggest that with the reduction of civil rights activism into the iconography of Dr. King (with his federal holiday
and with the memorial in Washington, DC), the impact of Jesse
Jackson's presidential bids in 1984 and 1988, and with the election of
Obama in 2008, what we witnessed amounted to a radical narrowing

of Black politics[69] in which the totality of Black political concerns seemed bound up with the relative success or failure of Obama's presidency. Alongside this narrowing of political action was a moralistic narrative of Black struggle that worked either to discipline dissent or justify criticism of the president's purported failures. Beneath the arguments and, in some cases, the vitriol, to paraphrase the late Bob Moses, was all this rot.

I asked this question in Chapter 2: What if the very condition for the possibility of heroic action has slipped from view, and we are left with Black bourgeois aspirational claims standing in for *all* Black politics? I now see that the question actually contained its answer. The firedrake, the dragon that calls forth heroic action, has now become, and perhaps it always has been, that very politics where the uniqueness of Black selves is lost in the representative claims of a select few who, perhaps unwittingly, strengthen the hold of white supremacy on our understanding of democracy. We must insist, especially in this moment, on the uniqueness of our own voices together, not as a form of adolescent individualism consonant with neoliberalism or as a crass response to a pessimistic outlook that sanctions self-interestedness but as part of the hard work of reaching for a higher self in pursuit of justice that deepens democratic life. Together, we must shatter the romance with the prophets and heroes of old and release our imaginations to usher in a different way of thinking and doing Black politics—of doing democracy. And, yet, we are still able to answer Baker's question "Who are your people?"

In a lecture at the Harvard Law School, Bob Moses talked about, among other things, something he called "earned insurgencies."[70] The students of SNCC, he explained, had done the requisite work close to the ground to garner the respect of Black farmers and sharecroppers such that they were willing to risk their lives alongside them. SNCC had "earned the issues they placed on the national table." They had "summoned up human dignity to confront psychological contempt, economic deprivation, and deadly physical assault." Earned insurgency is an extraordinary consequence of a politics of tending, an effect of receptive practices characteristic of Ella Baker's approach in which trust, courage, commitment, and love, rooted in caring struggle, inform our willingness to risk everything in pursuit of justice and shape practices that cultivate the capacities of all involved.

Ella Baker's democratic perfectionism calls each of us to a higher self in which our unique talents are deployed in the service of justice. For her, the distinctiveness of who we are is not lost in an overarching narrative of struggle with its attendant heroes, nor is it collapsed into some tenuous idea of Black interests represented by some Black prophet or leader. Instead, the richness and complexity of where we stand with others becomes the place from which a better world is imagined. We all have that capacity: to imagine a world beyond the horrors of now and to implicate a future in the very way we earn our insurgency and stand up heroically to the darkness of the current hour.

We are the leaders we have been looking for.

— *A Thicket of Thorns* —

You your best thing. . . .

TONI MORRISON, *BELOVED*

AT THE END of Imani Perry's extraordinary book *Breathe: A Letter to My Sons,* she describes her love of Easter, from the sacrifice of Lent to the passions of the cross and Resurrection. This confession follows a beautiful account of the challenges her boys will face in a world such as ours as well as her gentle and loving effort to hand over to them the beauty and power of their inheritances. She recalls singing the hymn "Up from the Grave He Arose" on Easter Sunday:

> *He arose, with a mighty triumph over his foes.*
> *He arose a victor from the dark domain,*
> *and he lives forever with his saints to reign.*[1]

Perry's account of the victory of Easter is the culmination of all that she wants to give to her boys: a kind of resilience and triumphant grit, an inheritance that equips them to face the storms, because, as James Baldwin said, the storms are always coming.

We are more than objects of racism, she tells them. Our lives are more than the wreckage and ruins left over after the plunder. She insists they tend to their interior lives, sit with their fears, and imagine themselves in the most expansive of terms. Grace makes room for this. "Follow your yearnings," she instructs. "Take time to strip yourselves down to the core, to the simplest of joys. It is a ritual of reorientation, a steadying, a sense of grace."[2] And do so, she lovingly suggests with each sentence, in the fullness of a tradition, of an inheritance, that is the wind beneath your wings. Know the answer to Ella Baker's question: "Who are your people?"

Perry begins the book with a response to the all-too-familiar American refrain that "it must be terrifying to raise a Black boy in America." With the first sentence, an echo of W. E. B. Du Bois's *The Souls of Black Folk* and in counterpoint to Ta-Nehisi Coates's *Between the World and Me,* she announces her response to such fears: "Between me and these others—who utter the sentence—the indelicate assertion hangs mid-air." She continues, "Without hesitation, they speculate as if it is a statement of fact. I look into their wide eyes. I see them hungry for my suffering, or crude with sympathy, or grateful they are not in such a circumstance. Sometimes they are even curious. It makes my blood boil, my mind furnace-hot. I seldom answer a word."[3] Hers is a different scene of instruction. We are not reducible to our circumstances, she tells us. We are more than the hatreds that threaten to consume.

She whispers to her sons, who are no longer excited about Easter baskets and dressing in seersucker and linen on special Sunday mornings, that "I will keep taking you [to Mass] because I know you will need *it* even if not precisely in this way: something in the wake of all this death; the eternal spring."[4] The intimacy and intensity of the passage reminds me of this moment in Baldwin's essay "Nothing Personal": "I have been, as the song says, '*buked and scorned*' and I know that I always will be. But, my God, in that darkness, which was the lot of my ancestors and my own state, what a mighty fire burned! In that darkness of rape and degradation, that fine, flying froth and mist of blood, through all that terror and in all that helplessness, a living soul moved and refused to die."[5] Perry gives her babies the armor of love.

The confrontation with the evils of our world and the madness that results demand something of us. Something more. Something rooted in a heritage that belongs to all of us: that eternal spring. This is not a guarantee that all will be well; that in the end darkness will give way to light. Spring always comes. So does winter. But Perry guides the eyes of her sons, and her readers, not only to what was but also to what is possible, to the "as yet" (to what could be), and that imagining becomes the basis for a different kind of orientation to the world, what she calls *a revolutionary possibility*.[6] We are more than our circumstances. We are more than what the world says about us. Just look at how we got over and fly!

Mine is an abiding faith in the capacity of everyday, ordinary people to be otherwise and in our ability, no matter the evils that threaten to overwhelm, to fight for a more just world. That faith isn't naïve or a fantastical evasion of the ugliness of human beings. It reflects my willingness to run ahead of the evidence, to see beyond the limit conditions of my current experience, and to ready myself to act on behalf of something not yet in existence. It is also part of my inheritance: a faith bequeathed to me by those known and unknown souls who survived the absurdity of the American project when they could have easily chosen death.

These lectures sought to ground that faith in a philosophy and a politics that affirmed the capacities of people to be the change agents we so desperately need. In 2011, under the spell of the Obama presidency, I did not want us to lose sight of our individual powers in the excitement and glamour surrounding a politician who would inevitably disappoint. I did not want to outsource our needs and desires, once again, to a political class interested, mostly, in its own well-being. Instead, I wanted us to see the revolutionary possibility in self-cultivation on behalf of justice: that in the effort to become the kinds of people democracies require—the kinds of people a racially just society demands—we transform our conditions of living.

James Baldwin insisted that the messiness of the world was, in part, a reflection of the messiness of our interior lives. This claim doesn't deny the workings of capital, or the power of oligarchs, or the pervasiveness of systems of racial oppression. That would be foolish and naïve. The two forms of messiness influence one another. Baldwin insisted, and rightly so, that human beings have a role to play. Not as mindless pawns moved about by unseen forces or by the inevitable march of history or by the hideously petty nature of life itself. Our choices matter because all is *not* settled. We matter, because we are reacting, experimenting, feeling, concerned with influencing the direction of our encounters in a way that will benefit and not harm, and those actions in turn shape our environments. As such, the question of who we take ourselves to be—a question of the character of those who are making choices—becomes a central feature of democratic practice. Baldwin believed, and so do I, that we have to become better people if we are to change the world. He believed that we *could* be better by "being always open to exploring the claims of different ends,"[7] of imagining a different way of living with others, and of doing the hard work ourselves of changing the world, not handing it over to so-called prophets and heroes. This is at the heart of Black democratic perfectionism.

———

Black democratic perfectionism is that effort at self-cultivation—of tending to the state of one's soul—in the context of a society shaped by the value gap that distorts and disfigures our characters. In the quest to be better under such conditions, matters of justice become critical to one's efforts to reach for a higher self because unjust arrangements and practices block the way forward.

In his book *The Fugitive Blacksmith or, Events in the History of James W. C. Pennington* (1849), Pennington, the first known Black student to attend Yale and the recipient of an honorary doctorate from Heidelberg University in 1849, clearly illustrates the point about unjust practices and self-cultivation. He wrote,

> There is one sin that slavery committed against me, which I never can forgive. It robbed me of my education; the injury is irreparable. I feel the embarrassment more seriously now than I ever did before. It cost me two years' hard labor after I fled, to unshackle my mind; it was three years before I had purged my language of slavery, and now the evil that besets me is a great lack of that general information, the foundation of which is most effectually laid in that part of life which I served as a slave. . . . If I know my own heart, I have no ambition but to serve the cause of suffering humanity; all that I have desired or sought, has been to make me more efficient for good. . . . But I shall have to go to my last account with this charge against the system of slavery, "Vile monster! Thou hast hindered my usefulness, by robbing me of my early education.[8]

Slavery drastically restricted Pennington's ability to cultivate his mind. It sought to reduce him to mere chattel and denied him civic standing. We see the shame and self-loathing that spurred him to be better and supplied the substance of his ethical criticism. We see the insidious workings of the lack of self-trust. It was against the evil practice of slavery and the world that justified it, which deposited these feelings in his gut, that Pennington sought to reach for a higher self and to make himself "more efficient for good."[9]

Among the darker souls of this nation, that struggle for a higher self under captive conditions can be seen across generations—from James W. C. Pennington to the young people, like Perry's sons and my own, struggling today in a world where concentrated power and hatred have distorted so much of what is meaningful and obscured so much of what is possible. Black democratic perfectionism insists on the role and place of this individual quest as a core feature of a creative democratic practice and radical politics that foreground the transformative power of everyday people. We are not slaves or the mere objects of anti-blackness. We are more than dire descriptions of a world predicated on our subjection, degradation, and death with no room for redemption. We are the inheritors of a grand tradition, confronted with a world on the verge of collapse, and what we do in the face of evils that threaten to consume us all in the fire matters for a new world desperate to come into being. It matters in our individual efforts to reach for a higher self to be the kinds of people that world needs.

I am not an Afro-pessimist. I have argued for years now, before Afro-pessimism swept through the academy, that the pessimist is perhaps best understood as an optimist who has pitched his ideals a bit too high, the equivalent of Voltaire's Pangloss desperately trying to find his footing because his garden was not enough. Given that ours is not the best of all possible worlds, the pessimist concludes, as the philosopher Arthur Schopenhauer noted, that our world must be hell, where we "are on the one hand the tormented souls and on the other the devils in it."[10] The pessimist has thrown up his hands and, in some ways, resigned himself to the impossibility of the world becoming otherwise and, inadvertently, has given license to unbridled selfishness.[11]

I do not want to suggest that the Afro-pessimist is best understood in this way—that the problem with the view rests with "pitching ideals too high." On a certain reading, one might wonder why they call themselves pessimists at all, given their calls for revolutionary action in response to their searing account of the world. But I do worry that the reductive view of Blackness (Blackness as social death) leads to a pessimistic conclusion about the resources available to fight for a better world. In this sense, the Afro-pessimist has thrown up his hands, because any action to remedy anti-blackness with the resources we currently have only reinforces anti-blackness.

As a pragmatist, I reject this view. Not so much because I am a healthy-minded optimist but because I understand that to act in the world involves suffering *and* possibility. This is the "double connection" of experience: it is "primarily a process of undergoing; a process of standing something; of suffering and passion, of affection, in the literal sense of the term."[12] It also involves our acting, reacting, experimenting, and tinkering with the environment: that what we do can, in fact, improve or transform our conditions of living. We are not stuck with a world where all is settled beforehand, and where we are left to sit on our hands to praise or lament.[13] Much more is required if a better world—if salvation, rightly understood—is to be had.[14]

I prefer the language of meliorism.[15] William James wrote that meliorism "treats salvation as neither necessary or impossible. It treats it as a possibility, which becomes more and more of a probability the more numerous the actual conditions of salvation become."[16] Mine is a faith that if we act intelligently and with imagination, we can change ourselves and our world for the better. But the outcomes are not guaranteed and are often provisional. The world is a fraught and vexing place, precarious and perilous, with a history that is a thicket of thorns. Acting in such a world is no sunny walk in the park. As James Baldwin wrote in *The Fire Next Time,* "To act is to be committed, and to be committed is to be in danger."

In my first book, *Exodus!,* I struggled with this reality and, please forgive me for quoting myself, but the point I made some twenty-five years ago still obtains:

> Sometimes we are at a loss as to how to respond to the disease, the dread, and despair in our lives. . . . But once we stop pondering God's intent or the meaning of the cosmos, once we stop thinking of liberation, say, as an ascent to a messianic kingdom and instead see it as an effort to leave Egypt and secure basic human dignity for ourselves and our children, we are then in historical time and confronted with the tragic choices of fragile human beings.
>
> Tragedy is an inescapable part of the moral exigencies of life. It involves principally the moral choices we make between competing and irreconcilable goods, and it entails the consequences we must endure, if we live, and the responsibility we must embrace without yielding to what Toni Morrison calls "marrow weariness." Tragedy, in this view, is not understood as preordained doom; rather, it depends on us and, to some extent, the choices we make.[17]

Such a view informs the meliorist: that the world can either be saved or it can go to hell or it can be just a bit better than what it is; it all depends on what we do. This view also undergirds the chastened voluntarism in Ella Baker's work. She had faith in the ability of ordinary people to fight for freedom without the comforting illusion that, no matter what we do, all will be good. That illusion is a child's conceit. In the end, to resist conformity and to struggle for a more just world does not require that we deny living amid "the wild beasts," as Frederick Douglass said. We must acknowledge that the persistence of evils often frustrates our effort at self-cultivation. Baker understood that, and she insisted we act anyway because a better world, if it is to be, depends on us and nothing else.

––––––––––

I have always found Toni Morrison's novel *Beloved* (1987) illustrative of the view I am commending.[18] Set in Cincinnati during Reconstruction, the story confronts us with characters like Sethe, Baby Suggs, and Paul D who are shaped by the horrors of slavery and desperate to hold back memories of experiences at the Sweet Home plantation, which inform who they take themselves to be and ominously shadow who they imagine themselves becoming. Denver, a child who was never a slave but whose life has been shaped by that experience and the hard choices it exacted from her mother (who murdered her sister, Beloved, to prevent her return to slavery), strains to imagine herself on her own terms. Haunted by history embodied in the ghost of Beloved, all the characters at 124 Bluestone Road struggle to reach for better selves:

> "Sethe," [Paul D] says, "me and you, we got more yesterday than anybody. We need some kind of tomorrow."
> He leans over and takes her hand. With the other he touches her face. "You your best thing, Sethe. You are." His holding fingers are holding hers.
> "Me? Me?"[19]

Morrison offers a relentlessly brutal picture of the context in which this desire for a better future is expressed and doubted. No one is left untouched. The psychical and physical toll of slavery cannot be left aside; its effects intrude upon and infect new experiences, even the experience of love.

Moreover, what white people have said and done frames any effort on the part of those tainted by slavery and its afterlife to believe they can be otherwise. But, for Morrison, that foul stench covers all involved. In a moment of dizzying doubt and clarity, the character Stamp Paid, who works on the Underground Railroad and helps Sethe to freedom, says, "Whitepeople believed that whatever the manners, under every dark skin was a jungle. Swift unnavigable waters, swinging screaming baboons, sleeping snakes, red gums ready for their sweet white blood." And, for him, "the more coloredpeople spent their strength trying to convince them how gentle they were, how clever and loving, how human, *the more they used themselves up* to persuade whites of something Negroes believed could not be questioned, the deeper and more tangled the jungle grew inside."[20] This is the world, with its assumptions about who we are and what we are capable of, in which Sethe asks Paul D the question "Me? Me?" in response to his loving assertion that she is her best thing. Doubt and despair threaten to consume. How could one expect otherwise?

But Stamp Paid turns the tables, and his insight about the vexed relationship between white and Black folk sets the stage for revolutionary possibility. It opens space for a different kind of imagining and a different way of acting in the world: "But it wasn't the jungle blacks brought with them to this place from the other (livable) place. It was the jungle whitefolks planted in them. And it grew. It spread. In, through and after life, it spread, until it invaded the whites who had made it. Touched them every one. Changed and altered them. Made them bloody, silly, worse than even they wanted to be, so scared were they of the jungle they had made. The screaming baboon lived under their own white skin; the red gums were their own."[21] The jungle of their making that entangles us all becomes the backdrop for the arduous task of self-creation. Stamp Paid says that the problem is not us, even if it is *in* us. The problem is them.[22] And that is Revelation.

My aim here is to hold off a certain pessimistic assumption that can arrest action or reduce our efforts to simply reproducing anti-blackness. Stamp Paid's insight breaks open space for a different kind of imagining, an epistemic eruption that allows for the possibility of a self not consumed with what *they* think and do, even as one must be intimately aware of the dangers *they* present.

Another critical moment in the novel involves an exchange between Baby Suggs and Denver. Denver has realized that the ghost is literally consuming her mother—that "neither Beloved or Sethe seemed to care what the next day might bring." She has decided to risk herself and to "step off the edge of the world" if Sethe is to be saved.[23] For much of her life, Denver's self-imagining has been bound up and warped by the cruel realities of slavery and her mother's act of infanticide. She has lived retrospectively, obsessed with the epic story of her birth: her mother's escape from slavery and the actions of a poor white woman, her namesake, who desired velvet in Boston and who helped bring life, her life, into the world. She has been comforted by the illusion that caring for the ghost of Beloved—that serving as a caretaker and protector of the wounds of the past—amounted to a meaningful life. Only to see the memories of the past swallow everything whole like a sweet piece of salt water taffy. Denver decides to wake from her slumber and seek help for her mother and, by extension, herself.

But she hesitates. The dangers of the world and of the people in it seize her imagination and feet. She cannot move. "Out there where there were places in which things so bad had happened that when you went near them it would happen again. Like Sweet

Home where time didn't pass and where, like her mother said, the bad was waiting for her as well." Denver remembers a conversation between Baby Suggs and Sethe, where her grandmother dismisses anything redemptive about white people and the world they have created. "Don't box with me," Baby Suggs tells Sethe. "There's more of us they drowned than there is all of them ever lived from the start of time. Lay down your sword. This ain't a battle; it is a rout." With those words ringing in her head, Denver cannot leave the porch. The nastiness of the world had grabbed hold of her heart. But then she hears the words of Baby Suggs, the grandmother who died pondering colors:

> "You mean I never told you nothing about Carolina? About your daddy? You don't remember nothing about how come I walk the way I do and about your mother's feet, not to speak of her back? I never told you all that? Is that why you can't walk down the steps? My Jesus my."
> But you said there was no defense.
> "There ain't."
> Then what do I do?
> "Know it, and go on out the yard. Go on."[24]

Here the past does not consume or occupy the imagination like a jealous maiden. Instead, Baby Suggs offers a realistic description of the world and its evils. Not to elicit resignation or a pessimistic outlook, but to inform Denver's decision to act in such a world. "Know it, and go on out the yard." Know that "the wild beasts" continue to rampage. Know of the pain and suffering of Black people—the soldered bones—that undergird much of our way of life. Feel it in the marrow and act anyway.

The past is transformed from a cage to funded experience. After hearing Baby Suggs's words, Denver says to herself, "It came back. A dozen years had passed and the way came back."[25] Those memories inform her choices as she sets out to save her mother. She begins to live her life prospectively, with a future in mind. But it is important to note that the call to act is not overburdened with an abstract idea of resistance or subsumed into a grand narrative of freedom and liberation. The injunction to act here is closer to ground; it is bound up in the effort to respond to those problems that gum up life as it is lived. It emanates from the power of love that has survived the ugliness of slavery and blossomed in the heart of a child who dared to imagine otherwise.

My faith in our ability to engage in self-cultivation on behalf of justice assumes the nastiness of life. Afro-pessimists remind us, or at least me, that we ought not succumb to the allure of neoliberalism's fantasies. I agree. But, like Baby Suggs, I say to them, "Know it, but go on out the yard." And do so knowing that we are not reducible to the circumstances of our living. Ours is more than ruin and rubble.

Americans currently find themselves, and there is no reasonable way to deny this, in a moment of profound crisis. The country is changing, and the substance of that transformation is not clear. Americans are divided, and those divisions go well beyond ideological differences. They cut to the marrow of the bone. Too often we see each other as enemies. Disagreement is saturated with contempt. Mutuality drowns in the bitterness of our public discourse. The sense of common purpose and public good has been thrown into the trash bin as we huddle in our silos. Race shadows it all. The great replacement theory, panic and terror around demographic shifts, assaults on voting rights and affirmative action, bitter debates about American history. We find ourselves living among men and women, once again, mad with the fever of a distorted view of liberty and willing to throw away this entire experiment in democracy as they cling to their racial fantasies. Hubris clogs the nation's throat.

The answer to the troubles in this country rests, as it always has, with the willingness of everyday people to fight for democracy. Not with the outsourcing of that struggle to so-called prophets and heroes but with the realization that the salvation of democracy itself requires, in part, "the creation of personal attitudes in individual human beings" that affirm the dignity and standing of all people. It requires that we understand that democratic flourishing cannot be "separated from the individual attitudes so deep-seated as to constitute character."[26] We must be the kinds of people democracies require.

With these lectures, I have tried to reconstruct a view of the prophetic and the heroic in African American politics with an eye toward democratic life. In the end, self-cultivation on behalf of justice isn't about manners, decency, or civility, but about an idea of virtue that American democracy desperately needs, because we are drowning among calloused hearts that refuse to change.[27]

Hatred gums things up, gums us up. From the beginning, this has been so. It blocks the way toward others. It straitjackets the imagination and places us behind iron bars. I find that insight in the tradition, rightly understood, that Imani Perry commends to her babies—the insight that blooms in spring. Baldwin wrote in "In Search of a Majority" that "to be with God is really to be involved with some enormous, overwhelming desire, and joy, and power which you cannot control, which controls you. I conceive of my own life as a journey toward something I do not understand, *which in the going toward, makes me better.*"[28]

It is "in the going toward" that salvation can be found. That imaginative leap, which allows us to see beyond ourselves and to reach for another. To be vulnerable, to tend and to love, to rip off the mask that blinds us to the beauty of the human being right in front of us. To recognize the distorting and disfiguring effect of hatred and fear, and the exacting power of love.

No matter how vague the invocation of love may be, it remains the one force that transcends the differences that get in the way of our genuinely living together. In one of his last essays, "To Crush a Serpent" (1987), Baldwin recounts his journey with and through religion and, along the way, casts aside the hypocrisy of the white evangelicalism of organizations like the Moral Majority. He knows what it means to predicate a sense of self and national identity upon hatreds, fears, and grievances. The flames of such fears and the scapegoats that must bear the brunt of the hate are meant "to exorcise the terrors of the mob." As Baldwin wrote,

> Those ladders to fire—the burning of the witch, the heretic, the Jew, the nigger, the faggot—have always failed to redeem, or even to change in any way whatever, the mob. They merely . . . force their connection on the only plain on which the mob can meet: the charred bones connect its members and give them reason to speak to one another, for the charred bones are the sum total of their individual self-hatred, externalized. The burning or lynching or torturing gives them something to talk about. They dare no other subject, certainly not the forbidden subject of the bloodstained self. They dare not trust one another.[29]

But the kind of salvation I'm talking about is not found in such tricky magic. Nor is it in some Heavenly bye and bye. "Salvation is not flight from the wrath of God," Baldwin declares, "it is accepting and reciprocating the love of God. Salvation is not separation. It is the beginning of the union with all that is or has been or will ever be." It is found *in the going toward,* evident in the politics of tending, and love is its carriage.

The rantings of a romantic madman? Perhaps. But this is the gift I have found in the tradition that is the wind beneath *my* wings. The world remains cruel, and the United States is especially maddening. But the words of the late Toni Morrison seem more resonant than ever:

> Of course there is cruelty. Cruelty is a mystery. But if we see the world as one long brutal game, then we bump into another mystery, the mystery of beauty, of light, *the canary that sings on the skull.* . . . Unless all ages and all races of man have been deluded . . . there seems to be such a thing as grace, such a thing as beauty, such a thing as harmony . . . all wholly free and available to us.[30]

Now fly!

NOTES

A Story

1.   I adapted this account from Cliffert Ulmer, a sawmill hand born in Florida, who told this story to Zora Neale Hurston. Zora Neale Hurston, *Every Tongue Got to Confess: Negro Folk-Tales from the Gulf States,* e-book (2001; New York: HarperCollins, 2009), 96–97.

2.   Toni Morrison, *Song of Solomon* (New York: Alfred A. Knopf, 1977).

3.   In Zora Neale Hurston's *Their Eyes Were Watching God,* Nanny tries to explain the breath and depth of concern for her granddaughter, Janie: "When you got big enough to understand things, Ah wanted you to look upon yo'self. Ah don't want yo' feathers always crumpled by folks throwing up things in yo' face." The irony, of course, is Nanny's act of protection ends up "crumpling" all of Janie's feathers. Zora Neale Hurston, *Their Eyes Were Watching God* (Philadelphia: J. B. Lippincott, 1937), 52.

Looking Back

1.   I still hear the voice of the four-year-old girl trying to comfort her mother after Philando Castile was murdered and can still see the image of Alton Sterling's son Cameron weeping as he cried, "I want my

dad," as well as the image of nine-year-old Judeah Reynolds witnessing George Floyd take his last breath.

2. Her YouTube channel remains active, an eerie example of the afterlife of someone killed by the hands of the police. https://www.youtube.com/c/SandySpeaks.

3. Eddie S. Glaude Jr., *Democracy in Black: How Race Still Enslaves the American Soul* (New York: Crown, 2017).

4. I take this formulation from Ralph Ellison, who writes, "Since the beginning of the nation, white Americans have suffered from a deep uncertainty as to who they really are. One of the ways that has been used to simplify the answer has been to seize upon the presence of Black Americans and use them as a marker, a symbol of limits, a metaphor for the 'outsider.' Many whites could look at the social position of blacks and feel that color formed an easy and reliable gauge for determining to what extent one was or was not American. Perhaps that is why one of the first epithets that many European immigrants learned when they got off the boat was the term 'nigger'; it made them feel instantly American. But this is tricky magic. Despite his racial difference and social status, something indisputably American about Negroes not only raised doubts about the white man's value system, but aroused the troubling suspicion that whatever else the true American is, he is also black." Ellison, "What America Would Be Like without Blacks," in *The Collected Essays of Ralph Ellison,* ed. John F. Callahan, rev. and updated (New York: Modern Library Paperback Edition, 2003), 586–587.

5. adrienne maree brown, *Grievers* (Chico, CA: AK Press, 2021), 26.

6. "A Poor People's Pandemic Report: Mapping the Intersections of Poverty, Race, and Covid-19," Poor People's Campaign, April 2022, https://www.poorpeoplescampaign.org/pandemic-report/.

7. James Baldwin, *The Evidence of Things Not Seen* (New York: Henry Holt, 1985), 17.

8. Mark Berman, Julia Tate, and Jennifer Jenkins, "Police Shootings Continue Daily, despite a Pandemic, Protests and Pushes for Reform," *Washington Post,* May 4, 2022.

9.   Walter Benjamin, *Berlin Childhood around 1900* (Cambridge, MA: Harvard University Press, 2006), 129.

10.   The image of the mean old rooster in Toni Morrison's *Beloved* comes to mind. Paul D helped him break free. I had some help too. Toni Morrison, *Beloved* (New York: Vintage International, 2004), 85–86.

11.   All these years later this is how I read the last chapter of my book, *In a Shade of Blue: Pragmatism and the Politics of Black America* (Chicago: University of Chicago Press, 2007).

12.   Emerson would use the metaphor of ascending stairs here. But, as Langston Hughes noted, "Life ain't been no crystal stair." So I aspire to fly with feathered wings!

13.   "Do not seek outside yourself." Ralph Waldo Emerson, "Self-Reliance" (1841), in Emerson, *Essays and Lectures*, ed. Joel Porte (New York: Library of America, 1983), 257. This line of thinking would spill over and eventually shape my reading of Du Bois's "Of the Passing of the First Born," which sits at the heart of Eddie S. Glaude Jr., *An Uncommon Faith: A Pragmatic Approach to the Study of African American Religion* (Athens: University of Georgia Press, 2018).

14.   Ralph Waldo Emerson, "Man the Reformer" (1841), in Emerson, *Essays and Lectures*, 140. Also see James M. Albrecht, "Saying Yes and Saying No: Individualist Ethics in Ellison, Burke, and Emerson," *PMLA: Publications of the Modern Language Association* 114, no. 1 (1999): 46–63; and Jack Turner, *Awakening to Race: Individualism and Social Consciousness in America* (Chicago: University of Chicago Press, 2012).

15.   Ralph Ellison, *Shadow and Act,* in *The Collected Essays of Ralph Ellison,* ed. John F. Callahan (New York: Modern Library, 1995), 47-340.

16.   Emerson, "Self-Reliance," 274.

17.   Here I am following the insight of Christopher Newell, *The Emerson Effect: Individualism and Submission in America* (Chicago: University of Chicago Press, 1996).

18.   Ralph Ellison, *Invisible Man* (New York: Vintage Books, 1952), 266.

19.   James Baldwin, *Nobody Knows My Name,* in Baldwin, *Collected Essays* (New York: Library of America, 1998), 135–136.

20.   T. S. Eliot, "Tradition and the Individual Talent," in *Selected Essays: 1917–1932* (New York: Harcourt, Brace, 1932), 4.

21.   Ralph Ellison, "Address to the Harvard Alumni, Class of 1949," in *The Collected Essays of Ralph Ellison,* ed. John F. Callahan, rev. and updated (New York: Modern Library Paperback Edition, 2003), 419.

22.   Ellison, "Address to the Harvard Alumni, Class of 1949," 420.

23.   Ellison, "Address to the Harvard Alumni, Class of 1949," 420.

24.   Ellison, "Address to the Harvard Alumni, Class of 1949," 423.

25.   John Dewey, *The Influence of Darwin on Philosophy and Other Essays in Contemporary Thought* (New York: Henry Holt, 1910), 17. Emphasis added.

26.   I reject how the linguistic turn in philosophy leads West to reject Dewey's view of experience. And I have sought to give Deweyan pragmatism a particular resonance through my engagement with African American sources. One can see this as I stage an encounter between Dewey and Toni Morrison's classic novel *Beloved* in Glaude, *In a Shade of Blue.* I should also say that the view of pragmatism developed in these lectures informs the writing of two small books, Eddie S. Glaude Jr., *African American Religion: A Very Short Introduction* (New York: Oxford University Press, 2014); and Glaude, *An Uncommon Faith.*

27.   Toni Morrison, *Nobel Lecture* (New York: Alfred Knopf, 1994).

28.   For Dewey, "that belief is without basis and significance save as it means faith in the potentialities of human nature as that nature is exhibited in every human being irrespective of race, color, sex, birth and family, of material or cultural faith." John Dewey, "Creative Democracy: The Task before Us" (1939), in Dewey, *The Later Works, 1925–1953,* ed. Jo Ann Boydston, vol. 14, *1939–1941* (Carbondale: Southern Illinois University Press, 1988, 2008), 226.

29.   W. E. B. Du Bois, *The Souls of Black Folk,* in Du Bois, *W. E. B. Du Bois: Writings* (New York: Library of America, 1986), 364–365.

30. James Baldwin, "Introduction: The Price of the Ticket," in Baldwin, *The Price of the Ticket: Collected Nonfiction 1948–1985* (New York: St. Martin's Press, 1985), xvii.

31. James Baldwin, "Introduction," xx.

32. Baldwin, "Introduction," xx.

33. Baldwin, "Introduction," xi.

34. Baldwin, "Introduction," xii.

1. On Prophecy and Dr. Martin Luther King Jr.

1.   Russell B. Goodman, *American Philosophy and the Romantic Tradition* (Cambridge: Cambridge University Press, 1990).

2.   Richard Rorty understood romanticism as "the thesis of the priority of imagination over reason—the claim that reason can only follow paths that the imagination has broken." Richard Rorty, "Pragmatism and Romanticism," in Rorty, *Philosophy as Cultural Politics* (Cambridge: Cambridge University Press, 2007), 105.

3.   Richard Bernstein, *The Pragmatic Turn* (Cambridge: Polity Press, 2010), 85.

4.   John Dewey, *Democracy and Education* (Los Angeles: IndoEuropean Publishing, 2010), 160.

5.   This may conjure thoughts of utopian discourses, but that is not my intention. In my view, Dewey's experimentalism requires that we give attention to method as much as to ends. As Dewey states, "The value of any cognitive conclusion depends upon that method by which it is reached." John Dewey, "The Naturalization of Intelligence" (1929), *The Quest for Certainty*, ch. 8, in Dewey, *The Later Works, 1925–1953*, ed. Jo Ann Boydston, vol. 4, *1929* (Carbondale: Southern Illinois University Press, 1984, 2008), 160.

6.   Much of this chapter is a result of an ongoing conversation over these many years with Cornel West, Jeffrey Stout, and the late Albert Raboteau. Stout's important book, *Blessed Are the Organized: Grassroots Democracy in America* (Princeton, NJ: Princeton University

Press, 2012) has been particularly important as well as Albert J. Raboteau's *American Prophets: Seven Religious Radicals and the Struggle for Social and Political Justice* (Princeton, NJ: Princeton University Press, 2018) and Cornel West's general corpus, especially his first book, *Prophesy Deliverance! An Afro-American Revolutionary Christianity* (Louisville: Westminster John Knox, 1982).

7.   John Dewey, "Authority and Social Change" (1936), in Dewey, *The Later Works, 1925–1953,* ed. Jo Ann Boydston, vol. 11, *1935–1937* (Carbondale: Southern Illinois University Press, 1987, 2008), 136. Emphasis added.

8.   Wendy Brown, "Neo-Liberalism and the End of Liberal Democracy," *Theory and Event* 7, no. 1 (2003): 4–5.

9.   We saw the effects of this view in the mindless debates over masks and vaccines during a pandemic that left over a million Americans dead. Those who refused to wear a mask or get vaccinated did so in the name of *individual liberty.*

10.   John Dewey, "The Lost Individual" (1930), *Individualism Old and New,* ch. 4, in Dewey, *The Later Works, 1925–1953,* ed. Jo Ann Boydston, vol. 5, *1929–1930* (Carbondale: Southern Illinois University Press, 1981, 2008), 75.

11.   Dewey, "The Lost Individual," 75.

12.   John Dewey, *Reconstruction of Philosophy* (Boston: Beacon Press, 1948), xxvii. I have chosen to focus on words like "individual," "prophet" and "hero," but reconstruction has a broader purpose in Dewey's overall philosophical approach. Colin Koopman does a great job of outlining three components of reconstruction as "meliorative transitioning"—that is, "a directed transition from a problematic situation into a situation that is relatively more determinate." Colin Koopman, *Pragmatism as Transition: Historicity and Hope in James, Dewey, and Rorty* (New York: Columbia University Press, 2009), 199. First, reconstruction takes place within a problematic situation, not outside of it. Second, its aim is to clarify problems at hand—problems experienced in the course of navigating our environments—with

resources "already furnished in that situation." And, third, reconstruction is temporal and historical: "This remaking of the old through union with the new is precisely what intelligence is." John Dewey, "The Crisis in Liberalism" (1935), *Liberalism and Social Action,* ch. 2, in Dewey, *The Later Works,* 11:37. As Koopman writes: "Reconstruction begins with a problematic past situation and fashions transitions to a reconstructed future situation." Koopman, *Pragmatism as Transition,* 198.

13.   Dewey, "The Lost Individual," 76. Emphasis added.

14.   Matthew Arnold, *Culture and Anarchy: An Essay in Political and Social Criticism* (New York: The MacMillan Company, 1924), 133.

15.   Nicholas Wolterstorff, *Divine Discourse* (Cambridge: Cambridge University Press, 1995), 48. Also quoted in Jeffrey Stout, "Walzer on Exodus and Prophecy," in *Ethical Monotheism, Past and Present: Essays in Honor of Wendell S. Dietrich,* ed. Theodore M. Vial and Mark A. Hadley (Providence, RI: Brown Judaic Studies, 2001), 322.

16.   Abraham Joshua Heschel, *The Prophets* (1962; New York: HarperCollins, 2001), xxix.

17.   M. Cathleen Kaveny cites James Darsey in this regard. Kaveny rightly notes that "the availability of prophetic rhetoric within a particular community depends on a bedrock sense of common values, on which prophetic speakers can ground their cause in a common dedication to moral righteousness." M. Cathleen Kaveny, "Democracy and Prophecy," in *Law and Democracy in the Empire of Force,* ed. H. Jefferson Powell and James Boyd White (Ann Arbor: University of Michigan Press, 2009), 37. Also see James Darsey, *The Prophetic Tradition and Radical Rhetoric in America* (New York: New York University Press, 1997).

18.   Ralph Waldo Emerson, "The Uses of Great Men" (1850), *Representative Men,* lec. 1, in Emerson, *Essays and Lectures* (New York: Library of America, 1983), 626. Our descriptions of persons as prophets are often eulogistic: something known after all has been gathered in or consequences have been witnessed. Indeed the use of the description in

the present occasions debate. Proclamations of "So-and-so is a prophet" are always countered with "How could you say such a thing?"

19.   Jeffrey Stout makes this point quite convincingly in his assessment of Michael Walzer's reading of the Exodus story. See Stout, "Walzer on Exodus and Prophecy," 329–334.

20.   Hence Max Weber's apt characterization of the prophet's vocation as a political office. See Max Weber, "Politics as a Vocation," in *Max Weber: The Vocation Lectures,* ed. David Owens and Tracey B. Strong (Indianapolis: Hackett Publishing, 2004).

21.   John Dewey, "Three Independent Factors in Morals" (1930), in Dewey, *The Later Work,* 5:288.

22.   Here we see the connection with Ralph Waldo Emerson. Dewey writes of Emerson: "History and the state of the world at any one time is directly dependent on the intellectual classification then existing in the minds of men. . . . There are times, indeed, when one is inclined to regard Emerson's whole work a hymn to intelligence, a paean to the all-creating, all-disturbing power of thought." John Dewey, "Emerson: The Philosopher of Democracy" (1903), in Dewey, *The Middle Works, 1899–1924,* ed. Jo Ann Boydston, vol. 3, *1903–1906* (Carbondale: Southern Illinois University Press, 1977, 2008), 187.

23.   John Dewey, *Reconstruction in Philosophy* (1920), in Dewey, *The Middle Works, 1899–1924,* ed. Jo Ann Boydston, vol. 12, *1920* (Carbondale: Southern Illinois University Press, 1982, 2008), 172–173. See Steven Fesmire, *John Dewey and Moral Imagination: Pragmatism in Ethics* (Bloomington: Indiana University Press, 2003), 56.

24.   As Fesmire notes, "Imagination in Dewey's central sense is the capacity to concretely perceive what is before us in light of what could be." Fesmire, *John Dewey and Moral Imagination,* 65.

25.   Fesmire, *John Dewey and Moral Imagination,* 66.

26.   George Herbert Mead's view of social genius comes to mind here. Mead argued that each of us has the capacity to make the communities within which we live different through the actions we take to secure and expand the ideals that animate our communal life. It is here that

we see the differentiation between the "I" and the "me." But it is also here that we encounter genius—those persons with an incalculable quality who "carry to the nth power this change in the community by the individual who makes himself a part of it, who belongs to it." Their efforts "make the society a noticeably different society." But Mead goes on to say, "*To the degree that we make the community in which we live different we all have what is essential to genius, and which becomes genius when the effects are profound*" (emphasis added). George Herbert Mead, "The Social Creativity of the Emergent Self," sec. 28, in Mead, *Mind, Self, and Society from the Standpoint of a Social Behaviorist,* ed. Charles W. Morris (Chicago: University of Chicago Press, 1934), 214–222. So the point is not to deny that there are unique and powerful people who walk among us and who, on occasion, become symbolic figures for us through the scope and significance of their actions. History is replete with examples of such people. The point is that we all have what is essential to their genius.

27. Thomas Alexander, "John Dewey and the Moral Imagination: Beyond Putnam and Rorty toward a Postmodern Ethics," *Transactions of the Charles S. Peirce Society* 29, no. 3 (1993): 384–386.

28. I should distinguish acts of moral imagination that directly affect social and political arrangements—those that are described as prophetic—from those that run the gamut of mundane living (even those that are momentous decisions of conduct). The prophetic function is thus social in its reach and critical in its thrust—reflecting the cooperative efforts of human beings to live together in right relation. We can also see, however, that the prophetic function can be used for ends that are not necessarily just or democratic. Someone can view democratic forms of life as repressive and imagine the actual in light of the possible. Our task here is not to fall back on the language of good or bad prophets. Instead, we should think about such matters in the context of a fully articulated experimentalism.

29. The prophet's work entails, in part, a concrete demonstration of natural piety.

30. See Ian Balfour, *The Rhetoric of Romantic Prophecy* (Stanford, CA: Stanford University Press, 2002), 18.

31. Rorty, "Pragmatism and Romanticism," 107. Emphasis added.

32. "The Indispensability yet Insufficiency of Marxist Theory," an interview with Eva L. Corredor in *The Cornel West Reader* (New York: Basic Civitas Books, 1999), 227.

33. Richard Rorty, "The Professor and the Prophet," review of Cornel West, *The American Evasion of Philosophy,* in *Transition* 52 (1991), 75.

34. Rorty, "The Professor and the Prophet," 75.

35. Hilary Putnam, *Pragmatism* (Cambridge, MA: Blackwell, 1995), 2.

36. Despite my concerns, I am quite sympathetic to West's view just as I am to what George Shulman sets out to achieve in his important book *American Prophecy.* Shulman argues, and here West would agree, that we should "interpret prophecy as an 'office' that involves making certain kinds of claims in certain registers of voice: as a messenger bearing truths we deny at great cost, as a witness giving testimony about the meaning and costs of conduct, as a watchman who forewarns of danger to forestall it, as a singer whose lamentations redeem the past for the present" George Shulman, *American Prophecy: Race and Redemption in American Political Culture* (Minneapolis: University of Minnesota Press, 2008), 231–232. This seems interesting, and familiar, as far as it goes. But, I am less taken with the idea of prophecy as *office* than I am with the notion of its *function,* something that ordinary people do in the context of inquiry (and, of course, that *doing* has everything to do with self-care—not in the narrow sense exemplified by neoliberalism but in terms of "what kind of person one is to become, what sort of self is in the making, what kind of world is in the making"—the effects of which can distinguish one as unique or special). John Dewey, *Human Nature and Conduct: An Introduction to Social Psychology* (1922; New York: Modern Library, 1957), 217.

37. Steven Fesmire, *John Dewey & Moral Imagination: Pragmatism in Ethics* (Bloomington: Indiana University Press, 2003), 65

38. John Dewey, "Creative Democracy: The Task before Us" (1939), in Dewey, *The Later Works, 1925–1953*, ed. Jo Ann Boydston, vol. 14, *1939–1941* (Carbondale: Southern Illinois University Press, 1988, 2008), 226.

39. I am reminded of Emerson's words: "True genius seeks to defend us from itself. True genius will not impoverish, but will liberate, and add new senses." Emerson, "The Uses of Great Men," 620, 623.

40. Cornel West, "Martin Luther King, Jr: Prophetic Christian as Organic Intellectual," in West, *Prophetic Fragments* (Grand Rapids: William B. Eerdmans, 1988), 11.

41. Sacvan Bercovitch, *The American Jeremiad* (Madison: University of Wisconsin Press, 1978).

42. Clayborne Carson, "Martin Luther King, Jr. and the African American Social Gospel," in *African American Christianity: Essays in History*, ed. Paul E. Johnson (Berkeley: University of California Press, 1994), 159-178.

43. Martin Luther King Jr., "The Strength to Love" (1963), in King, *A Testament of Hope: The Essential Writings and Speeches of Martin Luther King, Jr.*, ed. James Melvin Washington (New York: HarperCollins, 1990), 509.

44. King, "The Strength to Love," 509.

45. We can understand faith as the precondition of prophetic action—the running ahead of evidence. Without it we are not open to the possibilities placed before us by the imagination. Such options would not be live ones for that person without faith.

46. See Charles Long, *Significations: Signs, Symbols and Images in the Interpretation of Religion* (Minneapolis: Fortress Press, 1986).

47. Martin Luther King Jr., *Strength to Love* (New York: Harper and Row, 1963), 109.

48. William James, "The Sentiment of Rationality," in James, *Essays in Pragmatism*, ed. Alburey Castell (New York: Hafner, 1948), 22.

49. To understand King solely in moral terms is to render him, following Hannah Arendt, unpolitical in that it would suggest that his primary interests rest elsewhere beyond this world where the wrongs

have actually been committed. Hannah Arendt, "Civil Disobedience," in Arendt, *Crisis in the Republic* (New York: Harcourt, Brace, Jovanovich, 1972), 60–62.

50.   I explore this in Eddie S. Glaude Jr., *Democracy in Black: How Race Still Enslaves the American Soul* (New York: Crown, 2017).

51.   David Bromwich, *Moral Imagination: Essays* (Princeton, NJ: Princeton University Press, 2014), 26.

52.   Bromwich, *Moral Imagination,* 32.

53.   This is critical to contain the threat of imperial imaginings, when efforts annex the capacities / imaginings of others.

54.   John Dewey, "Moral Judgment and Knowledge" (1932), in Dewey, *The Later Works, 1925–1953,* ed. Jo Ann Boydston, vol. 7, *1932* (Carbondale: Southern Illinois University, 1985, 2008), 270.

55.   It enables us to see that heretofore unremarked feature of critical intelligence—what can be called critical participation, where tensions felt and lived can become the basis for transformative possibilities. Critical participation is that consequence of inquiry that enables us to engage problematic situations within unjust arrangements. For example, we choose to participate in the electoral process even though we are aware of the various ways corporate interests have captured elections, because our critical efforts may bring about fundamental transformation. Dewey writes: "Democracy is the belief that even when needs and ends or consequences are different for each individual, the habit of amicable cooperation—which may include, as in sport, rivalry and competition—is itself a priceless addition to life." Dewey, "Creative Democracy," 228. In his book, *Shadow and Act,* Ralph Ellison describes this crucial feature of democratic life as "antagonistic cooperation."

56.   Bromwich, *Moral Imagination,* 17.

57.   Shulman provides an excellent reading of this aspect of King. See Shulman, *American Prophecy,* ch. 3.

58.   Dewey, "Creative Democracy," 226.

59.   Martin Luther King Jr., "Facing the Challenge of a New Age" (1957), in King, *A Testament of Hope,* 141.

60. David Levering Lewis, "Martin Luther King, Jr.," in *Black Leaders of the Twentieth Century*, ed. John Hope Franklin and August Meier (Urbana: University of Illinois Press, 1982), 278.

61. Martin Luther King Jr., "Where Do We Go from Here: Chaos or Community?" (1967), in King, *A Testament of Hope*, 629.

62. Revelation 21:5.

63. Martin Luther King Jr., "Remaining Awake through a Great Revolution" (1968), in King, *A Testament of Hope*, 268.

64. Bromwich, "Moral Imagination," 32.

2. On Heroism and Malcolm X

1. James Baldwin, *No Name in the Street*, in Baldwin, *Collected Essays* (New York: Library of America, 1998), 354–355.

2. James Baldwin, "The White Man's Guilt," in Baldwin, *Collected Essays*, 722–723.

3. See Stanley Cavell, *Conditions Handsome and Unhandsome* (Chicago: University of Chicago Press, 1991); Jeffrey Stout, interview by Ron Kuipers, "Excellence and the Emersonian Perfectionist: An Interview with Jeffrey Stout, Part 1," *The Other Journal*, September 2009, https://theotherjournal.com/2009/09/excellence-and-the -emersonian-perfectionist-an-interview-with-jeffrey-stout-part-i/.

4. W. E. B. Du Bois, *The Souls of Black Folk*, in *W. E. B. Du Bois: Writings*, 364.

5. Toni Morrison, *Beloved* (New York: Vintage International, 2004).

6. Natasha Trethewey, "Native Guard," in Trethewey, *Native Guard: Poems* (Boston: A Mariner Book, 2007), 29-30.

7. W. Ralph Eubanks, *A Place Like Mississippi: A Journey Through a Real and Imagined Literary Landscape* (Portland, OR: Timber Press, 2021), 18.

8. Here I am in conversation with Ralph Ellison and his engagement with the hero. Ellison writes about Lord Raglan and his work on the hero: "I seem to recall that he noted about twenty-two aspects of character and experience that were attributed to most heroes, and he

discovered that historical figures . . . all tended to embody clusterings of these same mythological aspects, and this whether they were figures of fact or fantasy. Thus, it would seem that the human imagination finds it necessary to take exemplary people—charismatic personalities, cultural heroes—and enlarge upon them. The mythmaking tendency of the human imagination enlarges such figures by adding to their specific histories and characters accomplishments and characteristics attributed to heroes in the past." See Ralph Ellison, "Initiation Rites and Power: A Lecture at Westpoint," in *The Collected Essays of Ralph Ellison,* ed. John F. Callahan (New York: Modern Library, 1995), 524.

9.   Thomas Carlyle, *On Heroes, Hero Worship and the Heroic in History* (Lincoln: University of Nebraska Press, 1966), 115.

10.   See Barry Schwartz, *Abraham Lincoln in the Post-Heroic Era* (Chicago: University of Chicago Press, 2008), 187.

11.   Schwartz, *Abraham Lincoln in the Post-Heroic Era,* 17. See Friedrich Nietzsche, *On the Genealogy of Morals,* trans. Walter Kaufmann (1967; New York: Vintage, 1989).

12.   Schwartz, *Abraham Lincoln in the Post-Heroic Era,* 187.

13.   Ralph Waldo Emerson, *Nature,* in Emerson, *Essays and Lectures,* ed. Joel Porte (New York: Library of America, 1983), 7.

14.   George B. Forgie, *Patricide in the House Divided: A Psychological Interpretation of Lincoln and His Age* (New York: W. W. Norton, 1979).

15.   Wendy Brown, "Moralism as Anti-Politics," in Brown, *Politics Out of History* (Princeton, NJ: Princeton University Press, 2001), 30.

16.   Friedrich Nietzsche, *On the Genealogy of Morals: A Polemic,* trans. Francis Golffing (New York: Doubleday Anchor Books, 1956), 220.

17.   Schwartz, *Abraham Lincoln in the Post-Heroic Era,* 218.

18.   Schwartz seems to hold the view that democracy is antithetical to heroic virtue. But I agree with my colleague, Jeffrey Stout, that democracy "inculcates habits of reasoning, certain attitudes toward deference and authority in political discussion, and love for certain goods and virtues, as well as a disposition to respond to certain types of actions, events, or persons with admiration, pity, or horror." Jeffrey Stout, *Democracy and Tradition* (Princeton, NJ: Princeton University Press, 2004), 3. On this

view, heroic virtue is wholly possible in democratic life. I should add that if a "democracy engages in an ongoing interpretation of itself and an ongoing production of new practices and narratives, of new values and forms of social and personal life," as Rebecca Chopp notes, then the idea of the heroic should also be open to retrieval under different conditions and expectations. See Rebecca Chopp, "From Patriarchy into Freedom: A Conversation between American Feminist Theology and French Feminism," in *The Postmodern God: A Theological Reader,* ed. Graham Ward (Oxford: Blackwell, 1997). Also quoted in Stout, *Democracy and Tradition,* 6.

19.   Ralph Waldo Emerson, *Representative Men,* in Emerson, *Essays and Lectures,* ed. Joel Porte (New York: Library of America, 1983), 630.

20.   Emerson, *Representative Men,* 760.

21.   Emerson, *Representative Men,* 627.

22.   Emerson, *Representative Men,* 630.

23.   As Lawrence Buell puts it: "'Representative' was carefully chosen over against the Carlylean 'hero' in order to make the 'democratic' point that 'the genius is great not because he surpasses but because he represents his constituency.' Representative men are not authority figures but images of human potential." Lawrence Buell, *Emerson* (Cambridge, MA: Harvard University Press, 2003), 82. He quotes Perry Miller, "Emersonian Genius and the American Democracy" (1953), in *Emerson: A Collection of Critical Essays,* ed. Milton Konvitz and Stephen Whicher (Englewood Cliffs, NJ: Prentice-Hall, 1962), 82.

24.   Thomas Carlyle, *On Heroes, Hero-Worship and the Heroic in History,* ed. Carl Niemeyer (Lincoln: University of Nebraska Press, 1966), 20.

25.   Sidney Hook, *The Hero in History* (Boston: Beacon Press, 1943), 239.

26.   Hook, *The Hero in History,* 238.

27.   Neoliberalism has further distorted this view. Imagine the idea of the heroic in our current moment—we must have special powers or be superrich: Marvel's Avengers or DC Comics' Batman.

28.   Quoted in Robert Richardson, *Emerson: The Mind on Fire* (Berkeley: University of California Press, 1995), 58.

29.   I want to note that Cayton, Drake, and Ellison write against the backdrop of a generalized concern about the hero and Black leadership

during the 1940s. Ellison's work, for example, was informed by the very ways he answered the question: "What was there about American society which kept Negroes from throwing up effective leaders?" Also, a number of studies about the hero by scholars were published in light of the rise of figures like Adolf Hitler and Benito Mussolini, and FDR and Churchill. Sidney Hook's *The Hero in History* was written in this context. For an excellent treatment of this historical context, see John S. Wright's *Shadowing Ellison* (Jackson: University Press of Mississippi, 2006), ch, 2. For a glimpse at an important book that captures the tone and timbre of the decade, see Alvin Gouldner, *Studies in Leadership: Leadership and Democratic Action* (New York: Harper, 1950). Also see Lawrence Jackson, *The Indignant Generation* (Princeton, NJ: Princeton University Press, 2011).

30. Horace Cayton and St. Clair Drake, *Black Metropolis: A Study of Negro Life in a Northern City* (Chicago: University of Chicago Press, 1945, 1993), 395. One wonders how the ideal type of the Race Man distorts Black politics in the way that Adolph Reed suggests and how this is different from Ralph Ellison's aestheticizing of Black politics.

31. Cayton and Drake were well aware of the suspicion that racial zealotry might generate. In an astonishing discursive footnote, they acknowledge that the Race Man often warranted suspicion while the Race Woman did not: "It is interesting to note that Bronzeville is somewhat suspicious, generally of its Race Men, but tends to be more trustful of the Race Woman. 'A Race Woman is sincere,' commented a prominent businessman; 'she can't capitalize on her activities like a Race Man.' The Race Woman is sometimes described as 'forceful, outspoken, and fearless, a great advocate of race pride.'" Cayton and Drake, *Black Metropolis*, 394n. Here Cayton and Drake show some attention to the gendering work of race worker talk, complicating a bit Hazel Carby's claim that they uncritically contribute to "a rarely questioned notion of masculinity as it is connected to ideas of race and nation." See Hazel Carby, *Race Men* (Cambridge, MA: Harvard University Press, 1998), 4.

32. Ralph Ellison, *Shadow and Act* (New York: Vintage, 1964), xv.

33. Ellison, *Shadow and Act,* xvii.

34. *Journals and Miscellaneous Notebooks of Ralph Waldo Emerson,* ed. William H. Gilman et al., vol. 1 (Cambridge: Harvard University Press, 1968), 287-288.

35. Emerson, *Representative Men,* 628.

36. Albert Murray, *The Hero and the Blues* (New York: Vintage, 1973).

37. Ralph Ellison, *Shadow and Act,* in *The Collected Essays Ralph Ellison,* 59.

38. Manning Marable, *Living Black History: How Reimagining the African American Past Can Remake America's Racial Future* (New York: Basic Books, 2006), 153.

39. This rendering of Malcolm as icon also has the ironic effect of the demobilization of popular democratic energies by deepening the work of a certain kind of Black moralism (the disciplining work doesn't have to rely solely on King; it can also reach into the nationalist tradition to do its work). What is required is fidelity, not creative action. See Adolph Reed, "The Allure of Malcolm X and the Changing Character of Black Politics," in *Malcolm X: In Our Own Image,* ed. Joe Wood (New York: St. Martin's Press, 1992), 203–232. Also see Angela Davis, "Meditations on the Legacy of Malcolm X," in Wood, *Malcolm X,* 36–47.

40. Saint Augustine, *Confessions,* trans. R. S. Pine-Coffin (New York: Penguin Books, 1961).

41. James Baldwin, *The Fire Next Time* (New York: Vintage International, 1993), 67-68.

42. Arnold Rampersad, "The Color of His Eyes: Bruce Perry's Malcolm and Malcolm's Malcolm," in Wood, *Malcolm X,* 117–134.

43. Jean-Jacques Rosseau, *Confessions,* trans. Angela Scholar (New York: Oxford University Press, 2008).

44. Michael Eric Dyson, *Making Malcolm* (New York: Oxford University Press, 1995), 148.

45. "He was no prince; there are no princes, only people like ourselves who strive to influence their own history. To the extent that we believe otherwise, we turn Malcolm into a postage stamp and reproduce the

evasive reflex that has deformed critical black political action for a
generation." Reed, "The Allure of Malcolm X," 232.

46. Dyson, *Making Malcolm*, 183.

47. Octavio Paz, *In Search of the Present: 1990 Nobel Lecture*, Bilingual
edition (New York: Harcourt Brace & Company, 1990), 20, 32.

3. On Democracy and Ella Baker

1. See Clayborne Carson, *In Struggle: SNCC and the Black
Awakening of the 1960s* (Cambridge, MA: Harvard University Press,
1995), 20.

2. Ella Baker, interview with Gerda Lerner, "Developing Community
Leadership: Ella Baker," in *Black Women in White America: A Docu-
mentary History,* ed. Gerda Lerner (New York: Vintage Books, 1973),
352.

3. See Erica Edwards, *Charisma and the Fictions of Black Leadership*
(Minneapolis: University of Minnesota Press, 2012). Edwards offers a
trenchant criticism of the role and place of charismatic leadership in
African American politics and how it centers normative masculinity.
When I delivered these lectures, her book had not been published,
which includes criticism of my reading of the Exodus story in my first
book, *Exodus! Religion, Race, and Nation in Early Nineteenth-Century
Black America* (Chicago: University of Chicago Press, 2000). But my
concerns about the heroic anticipates much of what she argues. Although
I agree with her claims, I want to insist that Ella Baker was a charismatic
figure as well.

4. See Barbara Ransby, *Ella Baker and the Black Freedom Movement:
A Radical Democratic Vision* (Chapel Hill: University of North
Carolina Press, 2005), 188.

5. Baker interview, "Developing Community Leadership," 347.
Emphasis added. Baker evinces here a fairly widespread assumption
around the failures of the state to protect Black citizens from arbitrary
violence. She says in the same interview that during her time with the

National Association for the Advancement of Colored People (NAACP), her major job "was getting people to understand that they had something within their power that they could use, and it could only be used if they understood what was happening and how group action could counter violence even when it was perpetrated by the police or, in some instances, the state" (347). Also see Carol Mueller, "Ella Baker and the Origins of Participatory Democracy," in *Women in the Civil Rights Movement: Trailblazers and Torchbearers, 1941–1965*, ed. Vicki Crawford, Jacqueline Rouse, and Barbara Woods (Indianapolis: Indiana University Press, 1993), 8.

6.   Ralph Waldo Emerson, "Self-Reliance," in Emerson, *Essays and Lectures*, ed. Joel Porte (New York: Library of America, 1983), 259.

7.   Baker interview, "Developing Community Leadership," 351. Also quoted in Mueller, "Ella Baker and the Origins of Participatory Democracy," 64. Baker makes several points in this rather complex formulation. First, she notes *the pitfalls of Black leadership in a media age.* Baker's organizing preceded the advent of mass media as we know it. She worked in the bowels of the South, organizing membership drives for the NAACP when joining the organization could get you "beaten up or even killed." Obviously, the presence of television cameras (and their role in direct action campaigns) impacted and, in some cases, changed the nature of organizing. Second, Baker expresses how *the ascendance of media-driven leadership undermines mechanisms of accountability.* Cameras and coverage become the arbiters of who leads and who doesn't. Here one can see the residual trace of Du Bois's worry about Booker T. Washington. Not so much the concern over Washington's white patrons, but the very way his ascendance to leadership short-circuited accountability. Du Bois writes of the effect of Washington's leadership in *The Souls of Black Folk:* "Honest and earnest criticism from those whose interests are most nearly touched— criticism of writers by readers, of government by those governed, of leaders by those led—this is the soul of democracy and the safeguard of modern society." W. E. B. Du Bois, *The Souls of Black Folk,* in Du Bois,

W. E. B. Du Bois: Writings, 395. And, finally, Baker's suspicion about *the negative work of charisma* is clearly evident. Charisma can easily become the value. As opposed to a means to an organizing end, the charismatic figure can become the end itself and result, for example, in someone like Dr. King becoming the embodiment of the movement (this reduction of the movement to Dr. King, as Adolph Reed argues, would become orthodoxy by the late 1980s). See Adolph Reed, *Stirrings in the Jug: Black Politics in the Post-Segregation Era* (Minneapolis: University of Minnesota Press, 1999).

8.   See Ellen Cantarow, with Susan O'Malley and Sharon Strom, *Moving the Mountain: Women Working for Social Change* (Old Westbury, NY: Feminist Press, 1980), 55.

9.   Cornel West, *The American Evasion of Philosophy: A Genealogy of Pragmatism* (Madison: University of Wisconsin Press, 1989), 213.

10.   West, *The American Evasion of Philosophy,* 213–214.

11.   This is the source of my concern about his run for the presidency of the United States in 2024.

12.   Ransby, *Ella Baker and the Black Freedom Movement,* 270–271.

13.   James Baldwin, "The Uses of the Blues," in Baldwin, *The Cross of Redemption: Uncollected Writings,* ed. Randall Kenan (New York: Pantheon, 2010), 73-74.

14.   Here I am referring to Adolph Reed's brilliant insight about "the masses." Reed understands the term as a "homogenizing mystification." He writes, "It is a category that has no specific referent in black institutional, organizational, or ideological life. Unlike workers, parents, the unemployed, welfare recipients, tenants, homeowners, lawyers, students, residents of a specific neighborhood, Methodists, or public employees, the term 'the masses' does not refer to any particular social position or constituency. Nor is it likely that anyone consciously identifies simply, or even principally, as part of this undifferentiated mass. The category assumes a generic, abstract—and thus mute—referent. It therefore reproduces the nonparticipatory politics enacted by the mainstream black political elite. The masses do not speak; someone

speaks for them." Adolph Reed, *Stirrings in the Jug: Black Politics in the Post-Segregation Era* (Minneapolis: University of Minnesota Press, 1999), 16. Baker's insistence on *not speaking for but organizing with* distinguishes her view from the "massification" of Black politics (and that organizing was always grounded in some place and at some time in relation to specific problems). See Baker interview, "Developing Community Leadership."

15.   Romand Coles, "To Make This Tradition Articulate: Practiced Receptivity Matters, or Heading West of West with Cornel West and Ella Baker," in *Christianity, Democracy and the Radical Ordinary: Conversations between a Radical Democrat and a Christian,* ed. Stanley Hauerwas and Romand Coles (Cambridge: Lutterworth Press, 2008), 63. Also see Charles M. Payne, *I've Got the Light of Freedom: The Organizing Tradition and the Mississippi Freedom Struggle* (Berkeley: University of California Press, 1995).

16.   This is a critical point. John Dewey stated the point succinctly in a message read before the first public meeting of the Committee for Cultural Freedom in 1939: "If there is one conclusion to which human experience unmistakably points, it is that democratic ends demand democratic methods for their realization. . . . An American democracy can serve the world only as it demonstrates in the conduct of its own life the efficacy of plural, partial, and experimental methods in securing and maintaining an ever-increasing release of the powers of human nature, in the service of a freedom which is cooperative and a cooperation which is voluntary." John Dewey, "Democratic Ends Need Democratic Means for Their Realization" (1939), in John Dewey, *The Later Works, 1925–1953,* ed. Jo Ann Boydston, vol. 14, *1939–1941* (Carbondale: Southern Illinois University Press, 1988, 2008), 368.

17.   John Dewey, "Democracy Is Radical" (1937), in John Dewey, *The Later Works, 1925–1953,* ed. Jo Ann Boydston, vol. 11, *1935–1937* (Carbondale: Southern Illinois University Press, 1987, 2008), 298.

18.   Mary King in *A Circle of Trust: Remembering SNCC* (New Brunswick, NJ: Rutgers University Press, 1998), 25. Also quoted in Coles, "To Make This Tradition Articulate," 63.

19. Quoted in Ransby, *Ella Baker and the Black Freedom Movement*, 305.
20. Coles, "To Make This Tradition Articulate," 65.
21. More needs to be said about the connection between John Dewey's idea of critical intelligence and his talk of growth and Emersonian perfectionism. In a brief essay on Emerson, Dewey wrote: "[Emerson's] ideas are not fixed upon any Reality that is beyond or behind or in any way apart, and hence they do not have to be bent. They are versions of Here and the Now, and flow freely. The reputed transcendental worth of an overweening Beyond and Away, Emerson, jealous for spiritual democracy, finds to be the possession of the unquestionable Present." Here Dewey recruits Emerson into his own project. It is a strong reading of the Sage of Concord, but it offers an interesting point of entry into understanding how perfectionism might evidence itself in Dewey's philosophy. John Dewey, "Emerson: The Philosopher of Democracy" (1903), in John Dewey, *The Middle Works, 1899–1924*, ed. Jo Ann Boydston, vol. 3, *1903–1906* (Carbondale: Southern Illinois University Press, 1977, 2008), 190.
22. Robert P. Moses, "Constitutional Property v. Constitutional People," in *Quality Education as a Constitutional Right: Creating a Grassroots Movement to Transform Public Schools,* ed. Theresa Perry, Robert P. Moses, Joan T. Wynne, Ernesto Cortes, Jr., and Lisa Delpit (Boston: Beacon Press, 2010), 82.
23. See Wendy Brown, *Nihilistic Times: Thinking with Max Weber* (Cambridge, MA: Harvard University Press, 2023).
24. Richard Bernstein, *The Pragmatic Turn* (Cambridge: Polity, 2010), 81.
25. The appeal to the local is way of marking differentiated interests that have to be mobilized under specific conditions. One might think of this as moderated form of what Sheldon S. Wolin calls "centrifugalism." I say "moderated" because the idea is not to retreat into difference and eschew any idea of inclusive commonality. Rather, this form of localism takes seriously the specificity of place and history in the lives of particular individuals who constitute a community of

experience. See Sheldon S. Wolin, *Politics and Vision,* expanded ed. (Princeton, NJ: Princeton University Press, 2004), 586.

26. This could help us understand the decentralized character of the Black Lives Matter movement and its potential power.

27. Ransby, *Ella Baker and the Black Freedom Movement,* 370.

28. Sheldon S. Wolin, "Tending and Intending a Constitution," in Wolin, *The Presence of the Past: Essays on the State and the Constitution* (Baltimore: Johns Hopkins Press, 1989), 89, 90.

29. I am emphasizing here the formation of individual character that does not reach beyond the specific life in question but has political implications in that, for Baker, a person could take up the task of democracy: "Every time I see a young person who has come through the system to a stage where he could profit from the system and identify with it, but who identifies more with the struggle of black people who have not had his chance, every time I find such a person I take new hope. I feel a new life as a result of it." Baker interview, "Developing Community Leadership," 351.

30. Sheldon S. Wolin, "Norm and Form: The Constitutionalizing of Democracy," in *Athenian Political Thought and the Reconstruction of American Democracy,* ed. J. Peter Euben, John R. Wallach, and Josiah Ober (Ithaca, NY: Cornell University Press, 2018), 54–55.

31. Sheldon S. Wolin, "Fugitive Democracy," in Wolin, *Fugitive Democracy and Other Essays,* ed. Nicholas Xenos, 100–113 (Princeton, NJ: Princeton University Press, 2016), 100.

32. Wolin, *Politics and Vision,* 592.

33. Wolin, *Politics and Vision,* 603.

34. Wolin, "Fugitive Democracy," 107.

35. Wolin, "Fugitive Democracy," 112. Nicholas Xenos is right to problematize Wolin's use of "renewal" in this context. See Xenos, "Momentary Democracy," in *Democracy and Vision: Sheldon Wolin and the Vicissitudes of the Political,* ed. Aryeh Botwinick and William E. Connolly (Princeton, NJ: Princeton University Press, 2001), 34.

36. I am thinking of William James here: each ethical action amounts to a world unto itself.

37. Sheldon S. Wolin, "What Revolutionary Action Means Today," in Wolin, *Fugitive Democracy and Other Essays*, 377.

38. Sheldon S. Wolin, "Democracy, Difference, and Re-Cognition," in Wolin, *Fugitive Democracy and Other Essays*, 413. Emphasis added.

39. "Democracy does not complete its task by establishing a form and thus being fitted into it. A political constitution is not the fulfillment of democracy but its transfiguration into a 'regime' and hence a stultified and partial reification." Wolin, "Norm and Form," 55.

40. Wolin, "Norm and Form," 37.

41. Robert Lacey, "American Pragmatism and Democratic Faith" (PhD diss., University of Massachusetts at Amherst, 2006). Referencing Wolin, Lacey states that "perhaps we can best understand [democracy] as a rationally disorganized reaction against formal institutions and power structures." See Wolin, "Norm and Form," 37.

42. Wolin even hints at this:

> While it is of the utmost importance that democrats support and encourage political activity at the grassroots level, it is equally necessary that the political limitations of such activity be recognized. It is politically incomplete. This is because the localism that is the strength of grassroots organizations is also their limitation. There are major problems in our society that are general in nature and necessitate modes of vision and action that are comprehensive rather than parochial. *And there are historical legacies of wrong and unfairness that will never be confronted and may even be exacerbated by exclusive concern with backyard politics.* (Wolin, "What Revolutionary Action Means Today," 378; emphasis added)

This view raises the question of how democracy can be both local and national, and what might be the role, if any, of representational democracy in the face of such complexity. It is difficult to imagine what the answer might be for the latter, given Wolin's account of how representation disorganizes democratic energy.

43. Du Bois, *The Souls of Black Folk,* 381; emphasis added.

44. Jeffrey Stout, *Blessed Are the Organized: Grassroots Democracy in America* (Princeton, NJ: Princeton University Press, 2010), 254.

45. See Melvin Rogers, *The Undiscovered Dewey: Religion, Morality, and the Ethos of Democracy* (New York: Columbia University Press, 2009), 207. No wonder Wolin turns to Shakespeare's Hamlet. Wendy Brown argues that Wolin's invocation of Hamlet reminds us that "the cultivation of democratic experience in darkly undemocratic times will not vanquish darkness." Wendy Brown, "Democracy and Bad Dreams," *Theory and Event* 10, no. 1 (2007).

46. Stout, *Blessed Are the Organized,* 254.

47. The late religious historian Albert J. Raboteau criticized Hauerwas for this. In a conversation with me about Hauerwas's theology, Raboteau argued that American slaves who converted to Christianity exemplified exactly what Hauerwas commends, as they practiced their faith under captive conditions and, in some cases, under threat of death.

48. Sheldon S. Wolin, "Transgression, Equality, and Voice," in Wolin, *Fugitive Democracy and Other Essays,* 54.

49. Wolin, *Politics and Vision,* 604.

50. Brandon M. Terry has convinced me that this omission does not mean that the civil rights movement isn't doing theoretical work in Wolin. One could read the references to the movement in his work, Terry argues, in the way that Toni Morrison reads race in American literature. See Toni Morrison, *Playing in the Dark: Whiteness and the Literary Imagination* (New York: Vintage, 1993).

51. Juliet Hooker, *Theorizing Race in the Americas: Douglass, Sarmiento, Du Bois, and Vasconcelos* (New York: Oxford University Press, 2017), 30.

52. Sheldon S. Wolin, *Tocqueville between Two Worlds: The Making of a Political and Theoretical Life* (Princeton, NJ: Princeton University Press, 2003), 223–224.

53. Hooker, *Theorizing Race*, 32. She cites the DREAMers and Black Lives Matter as examples. One could also include the peaceful demonstration of the Southern Christian Leadership Conference. Bob Moses writes, "Like any Black person living in America I knew racism. What I hadn't encountered before Mississippi was the use of law as an instrument of outright oppression." Robert P. Moses, *Radical Equations: Math Literacy and Civil Rights* (Boston: Beacon Press, 2001), 58. Calls for law and order in response to their peaceful demonstrations precede Nixon's call for law and order. See Naomi Murakawa, *The First Civil Right: How Liberals Built Prison America* (New York: Oxford University Press, 2014).

54. Hooker, *Theorizing Race*, 32.

55. Henry David Thoreau, *Walden* (New York: Thomas V. Cromwell & Co., 1910), 11.

56. Eddie S. Glaude Jr., *Democracy in Black: How Race Still Enslaves the American Soul* (New York: Crown, 2017).

57. Following Dewey, who follows Aristotle, character should be understood as the interpenetration of habit.

58. My view of belief follows that of Charles S. Peirce: belief is thought at rest.

59. See Clarissa Hayward, *How Americans Make Race: Stories, Institutions, Spaces* (New York: Cambridge University Press, 2013).

60. Sheldon S. Wolin, "The People's Two Bodies," in Wolin, *Fugitive Democracy and Other Essays*, 381, 383.

61. Wolin, "The People's Two Bodies," 380. Xenos reminds us that Wolin borrows the idea of two bodies from Ernst Kantorowicz, *The King's Two Bodies: A Study in Medieval Political Theology* (Princeton, NJ: Princeton University Press, 1957): "Wolin carries over that fiction into the modern period. Since it was, in part, the fiction of the king's two bodies that made it possible for the revolutionaries of 1640 to execute the mortal body of Charles I while preserving his immortal body politic, the notion of two bodies in the American tradition suggests that it may be possible to kill off one body without damage to the other." Xenos, "Momentary Democracy," 28.

62. Xenos, "Momentary Democracy," 28.

63. This motivates a concern about Wolin's criticism of identity politics. Wolin writes:

> The ambivalence of identity reappears among many who consider themselves to be postmodern beings: they assert the value of identity as meaning individuality and—often at the same time—they proclaim the value of identity as sameness that is simultaneously differentiating and exclusionist, as in those who employ gender, race, ethnicity, or sexual preferences to construct a community of grievances or special qualities. The sameness that is used to establish the community then becomes the "difference" that distinguishes its members from nonmembers. Not infrequently it is accompanied by a demand that difference be recognized. The implication is that somewhere external to the community there exists a recognizer whose acceptance is deemed important because behind the recognizer is some collective identity, some association that has resisted extending the sort of recognition that the denied groups want because they feel threatened, diminished, slighted, oppressed, or because of all of the foregoing. (Wolin, "Democracy, Difference, and Re-Cognition," 409)

Much of the analysis turns on "recognition," and as far as it goes, I believe Wolin is right. But he fails to give attention to how "whiteness" functions (and how society chooses to generate power to sustain it). Without, at least some concrete attention to this operation, the criticism of identity politics rings a bit hollow.

64. Actually, Wolin finds the two terms inadequate. "Federalist," he writes, "fails to convert the radical nature of the position presented." And "anti-federalism" actually "wants to conserve, but it is driven to radicalism because there is no way for its conception of life forms to be maintained without opposing a system of power in which change has become routinized." Wolin goes on to say that "tending inclines toward a democratic conception of political life, intending toward an authoritarian conception as the nineteenth century understood the term: one who

loves the principle of authority, that is, the right to command and enforce obedience." Wolin, "Tending and Intending a Constitution," 88.

65. Wolin emphasizes the Tocquevillian point: "America was unique . . . as a land of political opportunity where individuals could practice becoming democrats. America's early political theorists in their eagerness to portray the American as 'endowed' with natural rights, fostered a myth that men [he should say certain men] possessed a kind of proto-citizenship prior to society. Becoming a citizen, they implied, merely confirmed a prior status. Tocqueville, in contrast, suggested that democratic citizenship had to be conceived differently, not as an antecedent or 'natural' status or even as a subsequent creature of law. Democratic citizenship was, instead, a process of becoming." Wolin, *Politics and Vision*, 596.

66. Sheldon S. Wolin, "The Liberal/Democratic Divide: On Rawl's Political Liberation," in Wolin, *Fugitive Democracy and Other Essays*, 261.

67. Cornel West, *The American Evasion of Philosophy*, 232.

68. James Baldwin talks about this model of leadership. For Baldwin, the Black freedom movement had upended forms of Black leadership that came into existence not so much because of efforts "to make the Negro a first-class citizen, but to keep him content as a second class one." James Baldwin, "The Dangerous Road before Martin Luther King," *Harper's Magazine*, February 1961, 40.

69. Much of this account is indebted to Adolph Reed. Reed's account of the transformation of Black politics post-segregation is breathtaking in its scope and prescience. See Reed, *Stirrings in the Jug*. We must also take into account how this narrative intersects with the development of neoliberal policies. See Adolph Reed, ed., *Without Justice for All: The New Liberalism and Our Retreat from Racial Equality* (Boulder, CO: Westview Press, 1999).

70. During the 2011–2012 academic year, Robert Moses, the famed organizer of SNCC, spent a year at Princeton. I was blessed to spend some extraordinary time with him. He delivered a lecture at Harvard

Law School sometime before his residency at Princeton and he gave me a copy of the talk. The quotations are from that talk. The idea of "earned insurgency" can be found in his essay "Constitutional Property v. Constitutional People," in *Quality Education as a Constitutional Right: Creating a Grassroots Movement to Transform Public Schools,* ed. Theresa Perry, Robert P. Moses, Joan T. Wynne, Ernesto Cortes Jr., and Lisa Delpit (Boston: Beacon Press, 2010), 83, 149.

A Thicket of Thorns

1.   Imani Perry, *Breathe: A Letter to My Sons* (Boston: Beacon Press, 2019), 148.

2.   Perry, *Breathe,* 147.

3.   Perry, *Breathe,* 1.

4.   Perry, *Breathe,* 148. This sentence carries the weight of a complex refutation of Christina Sharpe, *In the Wake: On Blackness and Being* (Durham, NC: Duke University Press, 2016).

5.   James Baldwin, "Nothing Personal" (1964) in Baldwin, *Collected Essays,* ed. Toni Morrison (New York: Library of America, 1998), 705. Emphasis added.

6.   Baldwin comes to mind, again: "And when a black man, whose destiny and identity have always been controlled by others, decides and states that he will control his destiny and rejects the identity given to him by others, he is talking revolution." James Baldwin, "Black Power," in Baldwin, *The Cross of Redemption: Uncollected Writings,* ed. Randall Kenan, 98–104 (New York: Pantheon, 2010), 100.

7.   Richard Shusterman, "Putnam and Cavell on the Ethics of Democracy," *Political Theory* 25, no. 2 (April 1997): 203.

8.   James W. C. Pennington, *The Fugitive Blacksmith or, Events in the History of James W. C. Pennington* (Frederick, MD: Aeterna Publishing, 2010), 35.

9.   Paul Taylor identifies some of the key tenets of moral perfectionism: "1. Character—insisting on the criticism and cultivation of character as

core elements of democratic practice 2. Self-criticism—interrogating the self, perhaps to the point of self-loathing as part of the work of ethical criticism and social activism 3. Shame (and the like)—mobilizing self-directed emotions as instruments for ethical self-criticism, especially as these highlight gaps between professed commitments and actual practice 4. Experience—recognizing the lived dimension of perfectionist practice, with its reliance on conditions like shame, as well as its temptations to despair, disenchantment and the like and 5. Experimentation—insisting that the transformation of selves in societies is an open-ended and dynamic process with no guarantee of success." Paul C. Taylor, "Moral Perfectionism," in *To Shape a New World: Essays on the Political Philosophy of Martin Luther King, Jr.*, ed. Tommie Shelby and Brandon M. Terry, 35–57 (Cambridge, MA: Harvard University Press, 2018), 42. Also see Chris Lebron, *The Color of Our Shame: Race and Justice in Our Time* (New York: Oxford University Press, 2013).

10.   Arthur Schopenhauer, *The World as Will and Representation*, trans. E. F. J. Payne, 2 vols. (New York: Dover, 1969), 2:573.

11.   The question I keep asking of Afro-pessimism is: What are its moral constraints? How might the pessimist respond to someone who concludes, given that Black degradation and death are constitutive of the West, that self-interestedness amounts to an appropriate response to anti-blackness? That an ethic of simply "getting yours" is the best response to such a world?

12.   John Dewey, "The Need for a Recovery of Philosophy," in Dewey, *The Middle Works, 1899–1924*, ed. Jo Ann Boydston, vol. 10, *1916–1917* (Carbondale: Southern Illinois University Press, 1980, 2008), 45.

13.   For Dewey, optimism "co-operates with pessimism in benumbing sympathetic insight and intelligent effort in reform." John Dewey, *Reconstruction in Philosophy* (1920), in Dewey, *The Middle Works, 1899–1924*, ed. Jo Ann Boydston, vol. 12, *1920* (Carbondale: Southern Illinois University Press, 1982, 2008), 178. Moreover, "it beckons men away from the world of relativity and change into the calm of the

absolute and eternal." See Eddie S. Glaude, *In a Shade of Blue: Pragmatism and the Politics of Black America* (Chicago: University of Chicago Press, 2007), 31.

14. I don't mean by salvation some final deliverance from sin or from harm. Rather, I am thinking about salvation as an ideal that guides our actions in the present with others—something to which we aspire like a world where we stand in right relation with one another. Baldwin comes to mind. "Salvation is as real, as mighty, and as impersonal as the rain, and it is yet as private as the rain in one's face. It is never accomplished; it is to be reaffirmed every day and every hour. There is absolutely no salvation without love: this is the wheel in the middle of the wheel. Salvation does not divide. Salvation connects, so that one sees oneself in others and others in oneself. It is not the exclusive property of any dogma, creed, or church." James Baldwin, "To Crush a Serpent," in Baldwin, *The Cross of Redemption: Uncollected Writings,* ed. Randall Kenan, 195–205 (New York: Pantheon, 2010), 203.

15. In my account of W. E. B. Du Bois, I treat him as a meliorist. Eddie S. Glaude Jr., *An Uncommon Faith: A Pragmatic Approach to the Study of African American Religion* (Athens: University of Georgia Press, 2018).

16. William James, Lecture VIII, "Pragmatism and Religion," in *Pragmatism,* ed. Bruce Kuklick (Indianapolis: Hackett, 1981), 128.

17. Eddie S. Glaude Jr., *Exodus! Religion, Race, and Nation in Early Nineteenth-Century Black America* (Chicago: University of Chicago Press, 2000), 166.

18. In Glaude, *In a Shade of Blue,* I stage an encounter between John Dewey and Morrison's *Beloved* in order to shift the center of gravity of pragmatism. I wanted to pull the philosophy across the proverbial railroad tracks. In this section, I return to that reading.

19. Toni Morrison, *Beloved* (New York: Vintage International, 2004), 322.

20. Morrison, *Beloved,* 233. Emphasis added.

21. Morrison, *Beloved*, 234.

22. I am reminded of a line in Simone Schwarz-Bart's hauntingly beautiful novel: "Long ago . . . a nest of ants that bite peopled the earth, and called themselves men." Simone Schwarz-Bart, *The Bridge of Beyond* (New York: New York Review of Books, 1974), 54.

23. Morrison, *Beloved*, 286.

24. Morrison, *Beloved*, 287–288.

25. Morrison, *Beloved*, 288.

26. John Dewey, "Creative Democracy: The Task before Us" (1939), in Dewey, *The Later Works, 1925–1953*, ed. Jo Ann Boydston, vol. 14, *1939–1941* (Carbondale: Southern Illinois University Press, 1988, 2008), 226.

27. Alluding to Romans 2:5.

28. James Baldwin, "In Search of a Majority," in Baldwin, *Collected Essays*, ed. Toni Morrison (New York: Library of America, 1998), 220. Emphasis added.

29. Baldwin, "To Crush a Serpent," 204.

30. Toni Morrison, "Moral Inhabitants," in Morrison, *The Source of Self-Regard: Selected Essays, Speeches, and Meditations* (New York: Alfred Knopf, 2019), 47. Emphasis added. Here Morrison quotes and riffs on a formulation from Annie Dillard's *Pilgrim at Timber Creek* (New York: Harper Perennial Modern Classics, 2007), 9: "Cruelty is a mystery, and the waste of pain. But if we describe a word to compass these things, a world that is a long, brute game, then we bump against another mystery: the inrush of power and delight, the canary that sings on the skull."

ACKNOWLEDGMENTS

In 2023, after fourteen years of service, I stepped down as chair of the Department of African American Studies at Princeton University. I was blessed over those years with amazing colleagues—some of the brightest minds in the country. I am especially grateful to Imani Perry, who has since made her way to Harvard University. When I wavered about delivering the W. E. B. Du Bois Lectures, she insisted that I not back out of my commitment. She gently prodded and poked at me to get started, and she read *every* draft. I also want to thank my colleague Joshua Guild, who attended all three lectures and, whether he remembers doing so or not, gave me detailed notes that I used in my revisions. April Peters, our department manager, made sure that everything ran smoothly when I caught the "fever" of writing. And Dionne Worthy, my assistant for so many years, kept my life from spiraling out of control as the pace of it all threatened to overrun everything. Shanda Carmichael now has that unenviable task.

Since the COVID-19 outbreak, I have been part of an ongoing reading group with a special collection of men: Mark Jefferson, Charles McKinney, Charles Petersen, Ronald Sullivan, Paul Taylor, and Cornel West. We started with Thomas Hardy's *Jude the Obscure* and have since read over fifty books together, and we are still going. They have been angels. Mark Jefferson and Paul Taylor offered detailed comments on the manuscript. Mark's pen made the book better. I am grateful for their generosity and insight. Hopefully I have responded to their criticisms appropriately on the page. I am also grateful to other friends like Jonathan Walton, John Lysaker, Kiki Denis, Farah Jasmine Griffin, and Melvin Rogers who took the time to read a draft of the book.

Cornel West continues to amaze me. I have given him every manuscript I have written since I was twenty-six years old. And each time he responds with affirmation and critique my chest swells and I smile. I hesitated a bit with this one, though. He is an object of criticism in the book, and I could only imagine how busy he was running for the presidency of the United States. But I decided to email him the manuscript anyway. The *next* day, at 8:30 p.m., he called and affirmed and critiqued. Words fall short. We have been having this conversation—this debate—for over twenty-five years. And my chest swells, and I smile, still.

Jeffrey Stout has been a crucial part of that conversation. I asked him if he could see our exchanges over the years in the book. He responded, "I can hear echoes of our conversations—like a Ciceronian three-character dialogue—reverberating on every page!" This book is better because of his detailed care with the manuscript. Over 180 comments. He has been doing this since my graduate school days. I didn't do all that Jeff asked, but his questions and provocations made the book better and suggest that we have much more to talk about.

Thanks to my wife, Dr. Winnifred Brown-Glaude, who has endured my craziness for thirty years. She tells me to rest and replenish. Another writing project lands on my desk, and my head travels elsewhere. Over the years, she has understood how important the work is to me and has given me the space, in every way, to live my vocation. Thank you for making this book, and every book I have written, possible. Given the difficult days in this country, I am blessed to have the support of my family: our son, Langston Glaude; my dad, Eddie S. Glaude Sr.; my mom, Juanita Glaude; my brother, Alvin Jones; and my sisters Bonita Glaude and Angela Glaude (who keeps me covered in prayer!) as well as my mother-in-law, Doreen Brown, and my father-in-law, Wilfred Brown, who has battled cancer like a champion over the last year. At eighty-nine years old he is still giving out "six love" on the domino table!

I owe an enormous debt to Henry Louis Gates Jr. for inviting me to deliver the W. E. B. Du Bois Lectures. Those three days were magical for a country boy from Moss Point, Mississippi. The staff at the Hutchins Center for African & African American Research were gracious and attentive. The lectures gave me an opportunity to make explicit what was going on in my head. Thank you, Skip, for giving me the occasion to fly!

This book would not be what it is without the care and attention given to it by the production team at Harvard University Press. I have to acknowledge the great work of my copy editors, Brian Ostrander and Paul Vincent. And *special* thanks to my editor, Sharmila Sen, who waited patiently for over a decade for this book and moved at the speed of light to make it a reality. I am so grateful and blessed to have had the opportunity to work with you.

———————

Much of the text of "On Prophecy and Critical Intelligence," published in the *American Journal of Theology & Philosophy* 32, no. 2 (May 2011), is reproduced in Chapter 1.

Since I gave the W. E. B. Du Bois Lectures in 2011, I have delivered versions of the themes in the book as lectures across the country. In particular, I want to thank Yale Divinity School and Emilie Townes for inviting me to deliver the Bartlett Lecture in 2016. This helped with Chapter 1. And thanks to Adam Sheingate and the Johns Hopkins University Project on American Pluralism for inviting me to deliver the inaugural lecture for the project in 2017. The material on Sheldon Wolin in Chapter 3 comes from that lecture.

INDEX

Afro-pessimism, 17, 72, 113–114, 120, 154n11

American Evasion of Philosophy: A Genealogy of Pragmatism, The (West), 15, 34–36

American identity: Black experience within, 15–16, 17, 38, 58–59; conscientiousness and accountability, 14–16; democratic values, 17, 38, 45–46, 58–59, 88, 121, 152n65; historical innocence and ignorance, 13–14, 120–121; identity politics, 59, 151n63; individualism and conformity, 22–23; white supremacy and racism, 5, 14, 17, 18, 100, 103, 120–121, 122, 126n4

American pragmatism. *See* pragmatism

American Revolution, and following era, 59–60, 99

autobiographical writing: of Baldwin, 10–11, 18–19, 50–51; of Douglass, 99–100; of Glaude, 48–49, 50, 52–53, 54–55, 71–73, 110–111; of Malcolm X, 54, 71–73, 74–76, 77

Autobiography of Malcolm X, The, 54, 71–73, 74–76, 77

Baker, Ella: Black democratic perfectionism, 8, 83–84, 89–90, 103–105, 107, 116; leadership, organizing, and pragmatism, 79–82, 83–92, 103–105, 107, 142–143n5, 143–144n7, 145n14, 147n29; politics of tending, 77, 80–82, 84, 91–92, 107, 147n29

Baldwin, James: autobiographical writing, 10, 11, 18–19, 50–51; on Black freedom movement, 7, 18, 152n68, 153n6; *The Fire Next Time*, 20, 75, 115; on love, 18–19, 42, 122–123, 155n14; *The Price of the Ticket*, 17–19; quotations, 7, 11, 18–19, 20, 48, 100, 115, 153n6; on salvation, 122–123, 155n14; "The Uses of the Blues," 84–85; on the world, 7, 11, 108, 109–110, 111, 121

Beloved (Morrison), 116–120, 127n10, 128n26, 155n18

Benjamin, Walter, 7–8, 33, 70

Black Christian tradition, 37, 38–39, 43, 44, 47, 149n47

Black custodial politics: alternatives, 110–111; described, and dangers, 5, 8, 60–61, 104–106, 144–145n14, 152n68

"Black democratic perfectionism": of
Baker, 8, 83–84, 89–90, 103–105, 107,
116; described, 8–9, 83, 111–112;
individuals' roles in, 2, 113, 121
Black freedom movement: Black
moralism effects on, 40–41, 61–64,
141n39; democratic parallels, 16–17,
38, 45–46, 87–88; events and time-
lines, 37–40, 45–46, 51–52, 79–80,
150n53; heroism and heroes of, 57,
58–59, 61, 71–72, 74, 75–76, 80; leadership development, 80–81, 86–87,
89–91, 106–107, 142–143n5, 147n29;
past views and reckonings, 7, 9,
17–18, 33, 37, 39, 60, 62, 76, 105
Black Lives Matter movement: democratic politics and, 8, 61; preceding
events, and founding, 4, 5, 125–126n1
("Looking Back")
Black Metropolis (Cayton and Drake),
67–68, 140nn30–31
Black political life: Black moralism
effects, 61–62, 64, 70, 141n39; Democratic Party assumptions and relations, 5, 8, 58, 61, 105–106; nationalist politics, 71–74; pragmatism, 15,
17, 79–82, 83–92; the prophetic and
heroic in, 22, 33–34, 37–41, 43–47,
58–59, 60–61, 67–68, 75–76, 80–82,
106. See also "Black democratic
perfectionism"; Black freedom
movement; Black Lives Matter
movement; Black Power movement
Black Power movement, 12, 57, 62,
153n6

Bland, Sandra, 4
Breathe: A Letter to My Sons (Perry),
108–110
Bromwich, David, 41–43
Brown, Michael, 4
Brown, Wendy, 23, 149n45
Buell, Lawrence, 139n23

capitalism: corporativist power described, 92–93; economic stratifi-
cation of, 46; neoliberalism, 22–23;
self-creation and -care amidst, 23,
53, 66–67, 111, 113
Carby, Hazel, 67, 140n31
Carlyle, Thomas, 56–57, 64, 65, 66
Carmichael, Stokely, 57
Castile, Philando, 125–126n1
("Looking Back")
Cavell, Stanley, 52, 53
Cayton, Horace, 67–68,
139–140nn29–31
charismatic leadership. See
heroes and heroism; prophetic
mode
Chopp, Rebecca, 139n18
civic participation: citizenship and,
99, 103, 152n65; "critical participation," 136n55; within democracy,
16–17, 87–88, 93, 103, 136n55; harms
of slavery on, 112–113
civil rights movement. See Black
freedom movement
Clinton, Hillary, 5
Confessions (Rousseau), 75
Confessions (St. Augustine), 74

conversion experiences, 71–72, 74–75
COVID-19 pandemic, 6–7, 130n9
culture wars, 57–58, 120
custodial politics. *See* Black custodial
   politics

Delaney, Beauford, 18, 19
democracy: American commitments,
   14, 16–17, 38, 45–46, 58–59, 88, 121,
   152n65; Baker and "politics of
   tending," 80–82, 84, 91, 106–107;
   body politic and political identity,
   101–102, 150n61; civic and critical
   participation, 16–17, 93, 103, 112,
   136n55; "creative" and pragmatic,
   43–44, 47, 82, 84, 86–89, 113; critical
   success factors, 16–17, 121, 138–139n18;
   Dewey's beliefs, 16, 29, 36–37, 43–44,
   82, 86, 88, 136n55, 145n16; equality
   vs. exceptionalism / heroism, 62–63,
   64–66, 80–82, 86–87; "fugitive,"
   92–100, 103, 148n39; neoliberalism
   and reconstructed individualism,
   23–24. *See also* "Black democratic
   perfectionism"
*Democracy in Black: How Race Still
   Enslaves the American Soul* (2016),
   5, 8
democratic localism, 88–89, 94,
   146–147n25
Democratic Party: Black America
   and custodial politics, 5, 8, 61,
   105–106; grassroots politics issues,
   148n42; national committees and
   conventions, 58–59

democratization: of heroic potential,
   64–65, 76, 77–78; of prophetic mode,
   8, 21, 29, 31–32, 34–35, 37, 47, 54,
   60–61, 80–82, 121, 133n26
Dewey, John: on democracy, 16, 29,
   36–37, 43–44, 82, 86, 88, 136n55,
   145n16; on Emerson, 132n22, 146n21;
   on individualism, 22–26, 29, 43–44;
   influence (on Glaude), 8, 15, 16, 22–23,
   128n26; moral imagination and
   critical intelligence, 20–22, 25–26,
   29–33, 41–42, 129n5; philosophy
   and pragmatism beliefs, 15, 16, 20–21,
   36–37, 82, 86, 128n26, 130–131n112;
   quotations, 20, 24, 42, 43, 86, 128n28
Douglass, Frederick, 63–64, 97–98,
   99–100, 115–116
Drake, St. Clair, 67–68, 139–140nn29–31
Du Bois, W. E. B.: on Freedmen's
   Bureau, 95; *The Souls of Black Folk*,
   143–144n7; "two unreconciled
   strivings," 17, 52, 69
Dyson, Michael Eric, 76, 78

Eliot, T. S., 11–12, 14, 78
Ellison, Ralph: heroism and
   "Renaissance Man" ideas, 67, 68–69,
   137–138n8, 139–140n29; speeches
   and social commentary, 12–14, 126n4
Emerson, Ralph Waldo: Dewey on,
   132n22, 146n21; heroic figure idea,
   48, 64–69, 70; influence, 8, 9–10,
   12–13, 14, 17, 40, 53–54; quotations,
   28, 48, 59, 135n39; "Self-Reliance,"
   9–10, 127n13

Washington, Booker T., 143–144n7
West, Alan, 61
West, Cornel: prophecy / pragmatism
  views, 15–16, 34–35, 82–83, 104,
  134n36; works, 15, 129–130n6
"What to the Slave Is the Fourth of
  July?" (Douglass), 97, 99
white privilege: American historical
  views, 5, 63; civil rights barriers,
  45–46
white supremacy: and American
  identity, 4–5, 14, 18, 72, 76, 103,
  120–121, 122, 126n4; as barrier to
  self-creation and heroism, 17, 68–69,
  70, 84–85, 117–118; criticisms and
  protest against, 4, 71–72, 90; growing
  and thriving despite, 108–110, 113,
  119–120; in political structures and
  parties, 5, 17, 18, 88, 103, 150n53,

151n63; racial habits and effects,
  100, 117–118. See also "other" and
  "outsider" labeling; police violence
  and killings; slavery
Wolin, Sheldon: fugitive democracy,
  92–100, 148n39; on identity politics,
  151n63; localism and centrifugalism,
  94, 103, 146–147n25, 148–149n42;
  politics of tending, 84, 91–92, 93,
  103, 151–152n64; on society and
  power, 101–103, 150n61
Wolterstorff, Nicholas, 27–28

X, Malcolm: *Autobiography,* and
  biography, 54, 71–78; as hero / icon,
  57, 70, 72–73, 74, 75–76, 77–78,
  141–142n45, 141n39; personal
  readings of, 10–11, 54
Xenos, Nicholas, 102, 147n35, 150n61